The Light and Love Within

FINDING CLARITY IN YOU

Shiena Gable

The Light and Love Within
Finding Clarity In You

Copyright © 2021 by Shiena Gable

All rights reserved. No part of this publication may be reproduced, stored in a retrieval system or transmitted in any form or by any means, electronic, mechanical, photocopying, recording or otherwise without the prior permission of the publisher or in accordance with the provisions of the Copyright, Designs, and Patents Act 1988 or under the terms of any license permitting limited copying issued by the Copyright Licensing Agency.

Published by
Shiena Gable
P.O. Box 75
Berry Creek, CA, 95916

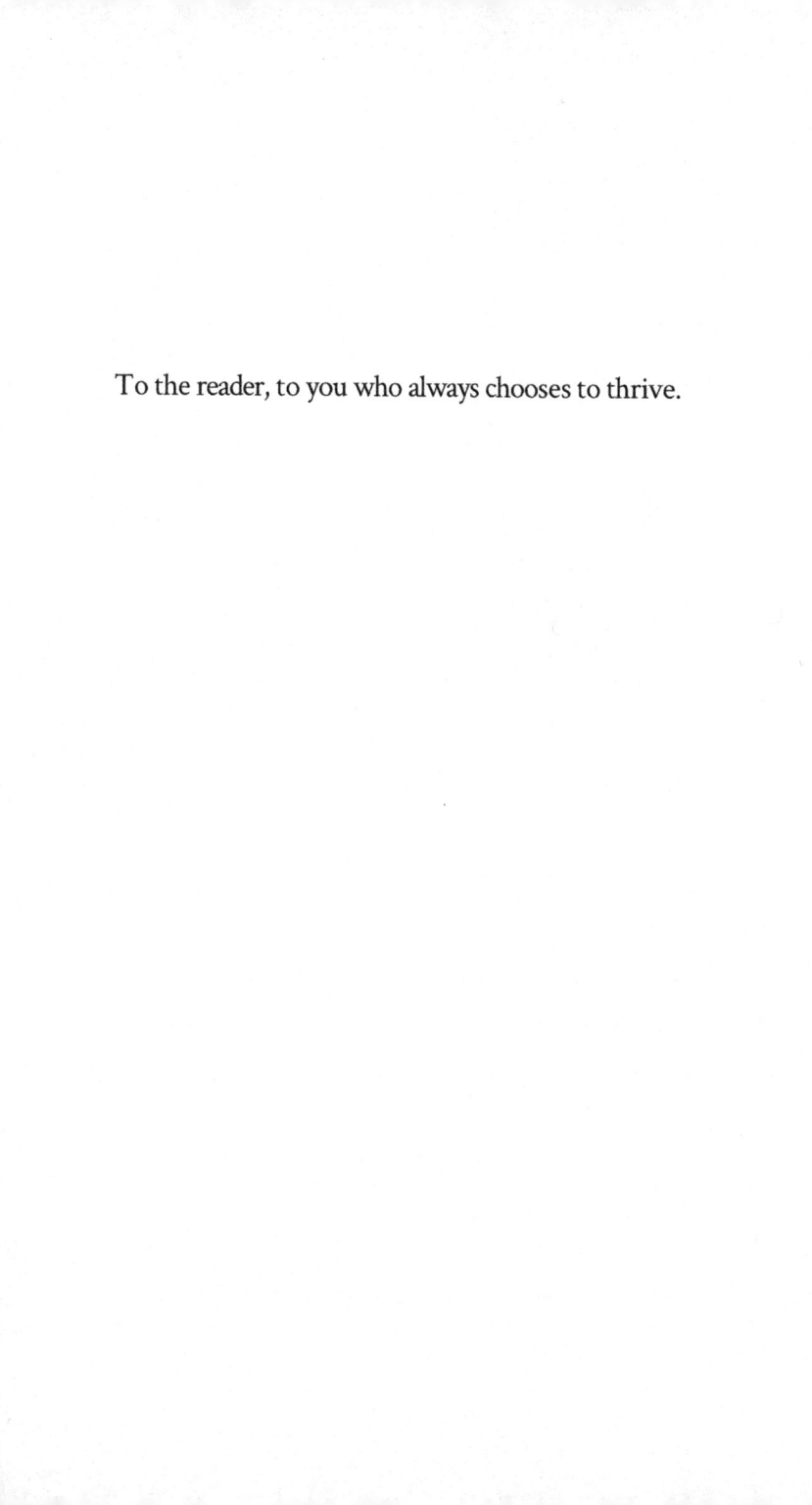

To the reader, to you who always chooses to thrive.

Table of Contents

CHAPTER 1
Self-Discovery & Awareness..................................5

CHAPTER 2
Planning the Life You Want..................................25

CHAPTER 3
Relationships..................................43

CHAPTER 4
Career..................................65

CHAPTER 5
Abundance..................................81

CHAPTER 6
Purpose..................................95

CHAPTER 7
Social & External Factors..................................115

CHAPTER 8
Spirituality & Physicality..................................125

FINAL THOUGHTS
The Journey..................................135

ABOUT THE AUTHOR..................................143

Preface

One morning as I was going through my daily routine, I went to the bathroom. It was past seven, and I had to get ready for work. I was there for a while as I gathered myself, washed my face, and prepared for the day. I noticed a very odd thing: three tiny dots vertically aligned on the door, almost as if they were projected onto it. I wondered how I never noticed them before? I got curious and went to get a better look. Upon closer inspection, I realized it was just the light coming through the window.

I looked at the window, peeked through the blinds, and saw how bright it was outside. I looked at the reflection again and thought about how, despite the brightness outside, so little light came through. I guess that, given the window was fitted with blinds, it made sense.

But as the day wore on, I kept thinking about that tiny reflection from the window. I wondered, "What if that light represents awareness? What if we are only letting in so little when the outside is as bright as it can be? What if we are not even aware of the blinds? What if we are not even aware of what we're letting in?" With all these questions, it convinced me to write a book, and so here we are.

I always felt that I would become a writer one day, but stayed away from that thought because I wanted to try other things. I remember being shy and very introverted; one reason I spent years expressing myself through writing. In my younger years at school, I'd just sit in a corner of the classroom and write about anything, and I found solitude in that—then and now. Writing has always made me feel safe because I could express myself without my prose judging me. But as I got older, I realized that I needed to try something else. I needed to find other ways to express myself.

I went on with my life, trying new things to discover what I might eventually want to pursue. I learned about video editing, photography, and at one point thought I wanted to be a news reporter. While I enjoyed discovering other possibilities, I was always drawn to the things that helped me express how I see the world.

When people ask what I do in my pastime, I always tell them I'm into photography. I like taking portrait photos. At first, I thought I liked it because of the creative process, or because I found it interesting, but realized it was mainly because I get to share what I see through my lens. When people say I made them look good in the photos, I tell them I didn't, and it was just how they look—and how I see them. It was in these moments that I finally figured out the way I perceive things is what makes me who I am.

I grew up in a small town in the Philippines, where life was simple but wasn't always easy. Growing up, when I found myself facing a problem, I always asked why. "Why do I have problems?" This question took me down a rabbit hole that made me view my reality in a different way. Since then, I never stopped believing there is more to life than what I think I know.

This book is a combination of every lesson in life that we forgot to identify and learn from. I hope you enjoy every bit of it and pick up something that you can eventually apply in your own life. Life is supposed to be fun, and it's not going to be unless we let it be. I am grateful for this opportunity, and I will always be thankful for having a positive approach to everything that I'm going through. By the end of this book, I hope you feel the same way, too.

CHAPTER 1
Self-Discovery & Awareness

HOW WELL DO YOU KNOW YOURSELF?

If you want to tell a story, it is best told from the beginning. If you want to live a life with better experiences, you first have to identify the YOU in that life. This kind of awareness is an internal knowing; the things you've learned about yourself on your own without the influences of others.

Who are you? What are you like? If you look at your life as if it was your physical body, self-awareness represents both your heart and your mind. That's how important it is! It is the core of what makes you who you are. It is the strongest foundation you can build, and it's also possible to rebuild it whenever the need arises.

My Opening to Awareness

On the last day of February 2020, I got up early and went about my daily morning routine, which includes a few minutes of meditation. While sitting in my home office as I waited for my computer to start, I heard a voice in my head for the first time. Initially, I figured they were just my thoughts, but the voice actually kept answering my questions. It was as if my mind was translating a conversation that involved two parties. That day I unlocked my clairaudience. It's a psychic ability in which you can hear your spirit guides, consciousness, source, or higher-self (it's referred to by many different names). Being able to hear my spirit guides was the greatest surprise of my life, and even if others may find it hard to believe, I know it's real based on my experience, and that's where I've decided to place my attention.

Hearing what they have to say has become a part of my day-to-day life, and I have asked them the greatest questions that have always puzzled me: "Why do I exist? Where do I come from? What happens when I die?" I was told that we exist because of love and that we come from love. When we leave this physical world, we'll have the answers to all the deep-seated questions we have about our existence. Since we still live in this physical world, why not enjoy every moment of it and not worry about from where we originated? It made sense to me in so many ways, and I'm not sharing this to convince you to resonate with it in the same way. At the end of the day, you can either believe what you want to believe, or believe what others want you to believe. You always have a choice.

CHAPTER 1: SELF-DISCOVERY & AWARENESS

Asking the Important Questions

Awareness is knowing your beliefs and having a clear understanding that only you can decide and settle on the set of beliefs that work best for you. Being aware is to be conscious of what makes you feel good in order to create the life you want to live. To help you start discovering more about your beliefs, here are a few questions to ponder:

- Who are you in your mind?
- Who do you want to become?
- Who are you in the dream version of yourself?
- What are your beliefs?
- What are your values?
- What makes you feel good?
- How do you like to live?
- What experiences do you want to have?

These are the questions many don't take time to answer, but they are the ones you really need to explore. I encourage you to get to know yourself better. After all, who else should know you better than yourself? When you know who you are, you will never feel lost. It's like having an anchor; you will always feel grounded.

Take this example. If you are a seed, but aren't aware you are a seed, you'll sit under the soil for some time in the dark, only seeing the earth, unsure of what's out there or what your future has in store. But if you identify yourself as a seed that grows, you feel secure in the knowledge that one day you will transform into the thriving plant you're meant to become. If you can choose between a belief that makes you feel limited or hopeful, why choose the one that limits you?

I know I've been throwing a lot of questions at you in this chapter, but I'm going to add some more because they are necessary:

- What are your actions like? Do they match your beliefs?
- What is your thought pattern?
- Do you carry negative emotions or positive ones?
- Do you believe in yourself?
- How do you perceive yourself, your life, your experiences?

Once you answer these questions, you will gain a better understanding of yourself, and you will also get an idea of what it is that you want versus what you perceive yourself, your life, and your experiences to be in this moment. You have to begin telling your story first by knowing who's telling the story; it's better than getting lost in all the plot twists.

Before you can "go with the flow," you need to first decide which flow makes sense for you based on your awareness of what lights you up.

The "flow" is your chosen path, and in this life you are exposed to various paths along the way. If you choose to go with the flow without plotting that path or understanding why and what's in it for you, you'll most likely end up going with the mundane flow that most people follow (social standards which focus more on the preferences of society rather than self). As a result, you become a follower, as opposed to being the creator of your life experiences.

When I was younger, I always felt there was more to life—that my life had a bigger purpose. Every time I think of that belief, it takes me to a different level of perspective. It helps me become an observer rather than the one experiencing life. I step back and look at things from a zoomed-out perspective. It has always worked for me because it taught me not to take things personally and not to remain too attached to outcomes—especially failures. When you try to see things from a wider lens you will have more room for solutions and not get caught up overthinking the situation. Learning to step back and observe doesn't get you entangled in the problem itself. This is one of the beliefs I hold on to because it helps me remain grounded.

Going Within

So, how well do you know yourself by now? What are the beliefs you have been carrying? Can you describe yourself beyond what you do in life, beyond what your family thinks of you, beyond how your friends see you, beyond who you are at work, and beyond what you are in the community? Who are you really?

Identify Yourself with the Good

When you are self-aware, you have clarity. You can easily define yourself according to how you see yourself; instead of how you were conditioned (i.e., how you were brought up and raised by your parents, taught by your teachers, seen by your society, acknowledged by your manager). This is identifying yourself beyond external factors and knowing yourself from within.

This internal knowing is understanding yourself for who you are, not according to the steps you took as a part of society or how others see you as (friend, brother, son, daughter, etc.); it's how you view yourself after facing personal challenges or celebrating a milestone. Who you have become after that harsh breakup, who you have become after your parents' divorce, who you have become after being homeless, who you became when you traveled the world, who you became after getting your dream job, who you became when your dreams came true for you. These experiences matter. You have to pay attention to them because these life lessons are transformational. If you look back and analyze your experiences, identify which felt good and which felt bad.

Then you can start sorting your experiences into categories, the ones that felt good—and the ones that didn't. I was doing this exercise a while back, and to my surprise, every experience I counted as bad was the reason why I'm in a good place now.

CHAPTER 1: SELF-DISCOVERY & AWARENESS

So I added a category called bad experience for a good reason. While they may have felt negative at that moment of the experience, how I perceive them now is positive.

I don't know if you've noticed, but the end goal of everything we do in life is to feel good. We feel good when we're surrounded by the people we care about. We feel good when we have freedom. We feel good when we are successful at something. We listen to music to feel good. We travel to feel good. We eat our favorite foods because they taste good, and it feels good. We feel good when we're secure. We feel good when we're healthy and when we are abundant.

So why does feeling good...feel so good?

I asked myself that question (I know, I talk to myself a lot), and I realized that feeling good —being happy, calm, content, and free—is what I believe to be my true nature. If I feel good that means I am embodying my most authentic self. I function well if I have a positive approach in life, and I like to identify myself as that kind of person. Every time I start acting and feeling the opposite of what I told myself I was, I start to feel bad. But because I'm self-aware, I can immediately tell that I'm feeling bad, not because of the experience I'm struggling with, but because I am disconnected from what I believe myself to be. That's why self-awareness is crucial, because not only will you feel when you get disconnected, but you will also know how to reconnect with yourself.

I explained that my true nature is being happy, calm, content, and free. When I feel the opposite of these emotions, I know I am disconnected from my true self. To reconnect with yourself, you have to engage in experiences that provide those feelings. It doesn't fix things right away, but what's important is that you focus on what you'd prefer to feel rather than what you currently feel. It starts with being aware of yourself because you have to know what makes you happy. For example: Eating ice cream brings you joy. So when you are sad and you want to change that, eating ice cream is that little step that helps you move away from that funk. If you know so much about yourself and have lots of ideas about what can make you feel good, then you'll always find a way to reconnect when you feel disconnected. This is also a way of comforting yourself, being nice to yourself, being a friend to yourself, and showing compassion to yourself.

One important thing to note is that having knowledge of who you are doesn't mean that your self-identification is fixed. It can always change, and when it does, you can make sure that it will be in your favor. I never judge myself if I need to re-identify according to new things I've learned, as this only means that I'm growing.

So if you can have freedom to identify yourself any way you want, then you can always choose to align with good. This ability allows you to have discernment around which beliefs you need to let go of and which beliefs need to be practiced. You don't need to carry everything, especially the bad thoughts. Identifying yourself with the good is as crucial as being aware of your own being. Your beliefs and thoughts are the foundation of your existence. If both of these are concretely built, your life will be as smooth as you wish and imagined it could be!

You need to know that you exist with the goodness of what this life has to offer—rather than the absence of it. When you feel bad, you know something is off; therefore, you gravitate toward what you identify yourself with, someone who feels good.

Take this example: If you believe you are lazy, being productive is going to be difficult because that is not who you believe yourself to be. But if you identify as being productive, when you notice yourself procrastinating, you remind yourself of who you are and can go back to being productive because that is what you know to be your true self.

Or, if you believe you are not good enough and someone shows you that you are, you won't believe them. Unconsciously you will end up showing them that you aren't, and the worst is you also reinforce your idea of not being good enough. If you believe you deserve good things in life, when faced with challenges, you have faith that the challenges will either pass—or turn into something good—because that is what you believe you deserve. By practicing this mindset, you not only become patient with yourself, but you also end up rooting for yourself all the time.

If you identify as a kind person, kindness becomes effortless. When you believe that you are love, hate becomes a stranger.

Believe In Yourself

Most of the time, we believe in ourselves only after others do. There is a certain feeling of encouragement when what you do is accepted by other people. And while there is nothing wrong with permitting others to say something about what they perceive, when you solely trust the path of your life depending on the opinions of others, you give away your power.

Once you become aware of your identity, you have a clear view of your belief system. With this knowledge, you can make sure that every belief you attach to yourself is something that can help you to become your best version. Believing in yourself and trusting that your own potential can take you somewhere should be something that is ingrained in you. You are the one who knows yourself best, and that's all the validation you need in order to succeed.

My Struggle with Believing

Prior to writing this book, I tried making YouTube videos as a way to share my ideas and inspire others. But I couldn't make it work because deep inside me were all these insecurities. I was always worried about how people would react. I was always conscious of whether they were accepting or appreciating the content I was sharing. So I ended up taking down my videos because I was clearly not believing in myself, as such, the message I tried sharing didn't come across. Even if my intentions were good, the disbelief I held with myself limited my voice.

When you believe in yourself, you validate yourself. You know your value, and outside comments represent nothing but words. You don't have to wait on someone or something to recognize your worth. The only approval you need is coming from within you. The people who resonate with you according to how confident you are will find their way to you and the people with whom you don't resonate will always have something to say—and that's okay.

Even if you are self-aware and identify yourself with the goodness this world can offer, it's all for nothing if you don't believe in yourself. If you have dreams, but you don't believe you can achieve them, your disbelief will pull you back toward thinking that you are not worthy. When you identify as a confident person, but you don't believe deep down that you are, then you become the opposite of confident. If you don't believe that you are unlimited, then you limit yourself.

Every time you trust yourself, you're expressing love for yourself. Every time you believe in your potential, you are appreciating your existence. Everything starts within you; what you believe becomes part of the reality you create. So stop expecting for something to happen and start believing it will. And never discount your inner voice again—there's a reason why you have it, so believe it.

Become a Creator

Once you've built a belief system that is in favor of your well-being, there's no question your life will skyrocket in a good way. The right mindset will take you to the next level. The pattern of your collective thinking is what you will manifest in your life. That's why it's important to discern which beliefs no longer serve you, so you can let go of the ones that hold you back from your deepest desires in life.

When people say, "You are the creator of your reality," it sounds too good to be true. At least, that's what I used to believe! I thought that even though it's a good thing, becoming the creator of my reality couldn't possibly happen. By becoming self-aware, I realized that with every yes or no decision I was already creating my reality! Prior to that, I believed that life took me where I was meant to go, and my job was to follow where it led me—I thought I should wait for the opportunities to come to me. Fortunately, I was able to drop that belief so here I am writing my book as I always dreamed.

There are millions of possibilities in this world happening simultaneously, and what you put your attention to becomes the reality in your world. Since you chose to put your attention to reading this book right now, this moment becomes your reality. In other words, what you prioritize becomes your reality.

So if you focus on the things, people, and situations that deliver toxic feelings, what reality are you creating? If your attention goes to things that make you feel less of yourself, what kind of reality are you expecting to see? If you home in on things that discourage you, can you expect an encouraging reality?

It's all about priorities. If you prioritize your well-being and the things that make you feel good, that is the reality that shows up in your life. If you stop giving attention to things that are not helping you, your reality shows you the opportunities that will.

Go After Growth

Have you ever noticed that when someone hits rock bottom it is usually when they think they are a victim of something? Most of the time, you think you're experiencing tough times because of reasons outside of you that you cannot control. Half of this is true since you really can't control situations, but what you can control is your reaction to them. But it's not entirely fair to say it's up to how you react to things because emotions can also become uncontrollable. So, how can you get out of victim mentality when you're facing hard times?

Imagine yourself believing that your purpose is to have an expansive life experience. If you go after growth, you won't take your problems personally because you know they are just steps to get you further on your path. With this mindset, you learn that your problems are not problems; they are opportunities from which to learn.

When you believe you are here to learn, you begin to see things from a larger perspective. You become a student of your experiences and not the victim of your problems. As a result, you become curious, wiser, and always choose to move forward because there's no other way. This also means you are less attached to people, situations, or things that don't lift you up. If, at some point you feel stagnant in your life, you know it's not you; it's just something about a lesson you haven't figured out yet. With this knowledge, you won't get stuck; and if you do, you won't beat yourself up for it. You will find solutions quicker and you will always look forward to the next lesson. When you treat every struggle as a lesson, you will not get hurt—you will grow.

Everything Starts Within YOU

When you see a painting in a museum, and you tell yourself it's not beautiful, what happens to the painting? Nothing. If you tell yourself that it is pretty to look at, what happens to the painting that very moment? Nothing. But how did you feel when you said it was not beautiful versus when you said

CHAPTER 1: SELF-DISCOVERY & AWARENESS

it was beautiful? You were able to react differently according to how you feel, but the painting remained the same. The painting will only be an attractive work of art or the opposite depending on how you describe it. This is how perception works. It's all about how you see and react to things. It's all about your point of view.

I was once invited to a birthday party where most of the people attending would be folks I don't know as well, leaving me to worry that I might not be able to relate to them. At least that's the thought that crept in. So before I headed to the event, I reminded myself that this wasn't about my worries, this was about me having fun. Of course, I ended up enjoying the party and having so much fun because I decided it would be fun for me. On the flip side, if someone else decided the party wouldn't be fun, they probably didn't end up finding it enjoyable. Because my perception of the party was fun, that became my reality.

The way you perceive things is very empowering. It's totally up to you. So if you decide to look at a painting and identify it as beautiful, then maybe you can also see your life in a positive light. If I can decide to have fun at a party, maybe you can also decide for your life to have the same experience.

Your mindset toward how you see yourself, how you trust yourself, how you love yourself, how you believe in yourself, and where you see yourself is the foundation of success in every angle you can find. If the way you think about everything affects your reality, then why would you let yourself think of something else aside from good?

Remember: You are powerful, so allow yourself to be.

Define Success and Become It

In the previous section, I brushed upon the idea of success. How do you define success? To me, it means achieving a goal I set for myself. Success is vague and subjective, and what it means varies from person to person. Some may define it as being wealthy and famous, some may say it boils down to having peace of mind or being in a healthy and loving relationship. In order for you to claim success, you have to define what it means to you first.

The reason most people beat themselves up for being unsuccessful is that they are unconsciously basing their definition of success on something outside of themselves. If you look inward, you will discover that success goes deeper than the usual standards of society. In addition, it's not always something we have to reach for, because success can also be found within. My main goal is to learn through life and have fun in the process. If I get another day to live to accomplish that, I'd be fulfilled and grateful. The secret is to learn how to disentangle yourself from other people's standards. Instead, set your own definitions according to your perspectives.

CHAPTER 1: SELF-DISCOVERY & AWARENESS

The more you try to shape yourself according to how others see things, the more behind you feel because you're running after someone else's point of view. You're an individual with your own perception; your own take on things. In addition, try to avoid crafting your definition of success based on others' recognition. Realize that every little win you have is something for which you can be proud. Your perception of things creates your reality, so set your own meaning of success—be it, live it.

Dispelling Societal Myths

We've always been told we need something to complete us. We are born into a society that values achievements measured by outside validation. We're told the grass is greener and richer somewhere, but we were never told that who we are is enough. That what we have within us is enough, and that by nurturing that, the rest will fall into place accordingly. Make it a point to always look after yourself and focus on what makes you feel good. This will help you find the truth in the things that light you up.

You are the key to that treasure chest you've been wanting to open, so I hope you feel empowered by the amount of magic that is lying within you. You can be who you want to be, so let yourself believe in your possibilities.

Once you master introspection, it is easier for you to navigate life and become a creator. When you are self-aware, you know that attaching yourself to the good side of it all is a remarkable way of living your life. If self-identification has become clear to you, you'll eventually build your own foundation that will be marking the starting point of where you should go with your life. When there's self-awareness, there is love and you function with it in all areas of your life experience—not because love is good but because you ARE love. It's the beginning of an incredible human experience that no material possession can replace.

Self-awareness also will serve as a grounding point from which you can practice humility and trust that you are safe. With your power to analyze and observe, it's easier to gain clarity to your life's purpose. There's no greater feeling than being able to have an awareness of what and who you are in a place where the answers aren't given. The answer isn't out there—it's within you. If you practice self-awareness, solutions come faster, and even before you start feeling lost, you will find yourself.

If you're reading this and still aren't sure what all this self-awareness stuff means, go to a place where you can observe people without judgment. Simply observe without distraction and practice it repeatedly. Eventually, once you feel as if you are able to watch others from a neutral place, try turning this technique on yourself, observe without judgment to see who you are in your mind and in your perception. It's important to remember that when you practice meditation, you quiet your mind and begin to become more mindful of the way your thoughts are processed. When you turn meditation into a habit, you will master your sense of awareness. This not only helps you become accepting of and inspired by who you are, but you will show up for other people in a more meaningful way. Another form of practicing self-awareness is to go for a nature walk and focus on seeing and appreciating the beauty all around you. Let go of distractions and make sure to put more of your attention on soaking in nature's beauty. Being present with an appreciation of such a magical creation from the divine will empower you, recharge you, and give you hope.

CHAPTER 2

Planning the Life You Want

THE VALUE OF SETTING INTENTIONS

In this chapter, you will learn about the importance of knowing what you want. When you have practiced self-discovery, it is easier to plan the life you want, because you know who you are and what you want to experience in your time here. Don't judge yourself if sometimes you tend to be the "I don't know" kind of person; instead, believe that you can become more by allowing yourself to be. Only limit yourself when it comes to things that aren't aligned with your values. If you are clear on your desires, take action and make them happen.

Have you ever had that feeling when you know you are not where you're supposed to be, but at the same time you don't know where you should be? I've experienced that a couple of times in my life and that is how I learned to take risks. I used to believe that if I didn't take risks, I wouldn't find what I was seeking, and I wouldn't break the current pattern keeping me stuck. Only later did I discover that I can do these things without risking too much or messing up what I already have. Planning the life I wanted was never my strong suit. Yes, I did set a few New Year's resolutions here and there, but with all the distractions in a year, I'd barely remember what I set for myself. In this chapter, I'm going to share my views on how to commit to identifying the life you want—and why it's important.

Carving Out Space to Plan

When planning the life you want, it is important to acknowledge where you're currently at, and identify the direction in which you want to go. Who are you at the moment? What are the things you do right now that inspire you? In this process, make knowing yourself and what makes you happy your priority. If you have no clue what you want right now, it's okay, but you might want to step back from your normal routine, pause for a while, and focus on yourself to achieve clarity.

Going Within

If you don't have clarity around who you are, there's really nowhere to go. If this happens, you may feel lost with a victim-mentality toward life. You can become bitter and, at the same time, accepting of the fact that you're not the creator of your life and everyone else who is succeeding in life is "better" (or luckier) than you.

CHAPTER 2: PLANNING THE LIFE YOU WANT

This is why you want to carve out the time to get clear. To achieve clarity in terms of planning the life you want, consider the following questions:

- Why are you planning the life you want?
- Why is it important to you?
- How are you going to plan it? What steps can you take?
- How important it is to plan your life?

By having more time to reflect on previous experiences, you can better gauge what it is that you desire. Having a vision of what you want your life to look like can prevent you from repeating mistakes and it will also help you prioritize things. Pay more attention to yourself in the present moment, and it'll eventually pay off in every area of your life!

Too Much Noise

For quite some time, I'd been extremely active on my social media accounts. I've been on it for 10 years and, I'd spend like six to nine hours a day just scrolling through posts. It was no longer healthy, so I finally decided to minimize the time I spent online. Social media is definitely convenient to see how my friends and family are doing, but at some point it became too noisy. There was too much information to consume, so I decided that instead of unnecessarily scrolling through my news feed, I could read a self-help book and that would be a more productive investment of my time. I could always connect with the people I care about by messaging them personally, so giving so much of my precious time to social media no longer made sense.

As I spend less and less time on my phone, I realize that from the time I was young, I've been bombarded with information outside of me such as TV shows, internet games, and social media. It was normal because that was what everyone I knew did! I didn't even realize I could quiet my mind to listen to my thoughts because most of the time I was just accepting ideas from outside sources. By the start of 2020, I made a commitment to become free from all social media platforms in the sense that I will only use them for my own good. I chose to pay more attention to myself and learned to filter the kind of information I consume. I started meditating in the morning and before bed. With this practice, I can easily identify which thought is mine and which thoughts don't belong to me. Plenty of beliefs and thought patterns are available everywhere, including in the books you're reading, the speeches you listen to, the shows you watch, etc. But you will never have a strong conviction around which beliefs you take in are good or bad for you—not until you take time for yourself and deeply evaluate these things.

There's a fine line between doing what you feel like doing versus doing something because you're so used to doing it to the point that you don't even know why you're doing it; it just became a habit and part of your routine. Your ability to know how you feel and gravitate toward what makes you feel good is one of your strengths. If you let others take that away from you, it's like you're giving your power away. When you step back and carve out time dedicated solely for yourself without any distractions, you will awaken to this truth. For a very long time, I thought I enjoyed going on social media, but later I realized it was more of an addiction rather than my own will to be on it. I'm not saying it's bad for you; I'm saying it's important to have a reason to be on it and be aware of that reason when you're online. Once you become blind to your reasoning, it can become addictive.

The "Why" and the "How"

The deeper you know yourself, the more fulfilling your existence becomes, and the more you listen to your thoughts, the clearer your path becomes. What kind of person do you want to become? Asking this is another way to identify where you're at in your life and where you want it to take you. If you want to become a wealthy person, you need to take action to get there so it makes sense to start learning about finances, investments, and any businesses that can generate good income. If you want to become a good singer, then singing more, enrolling in a voice class, or working with a vocal coach makes sense. If you want to become an optimistic person, then one of the steps might be to look for self-help books on this topic or to take more time to reflect and learn from your own experiences. When you identify what you want to do, the steps to get there often present themselves.

The "When"

There's no specific time or date as to when you should decide on your path; it's entirely up to you. Many people wake up and realize they are not living the life they want only after they hit rock bottom, when they experienced the lowest point of their lives. But you don't have to wait to lose a job, lose someone you love, or lose yourself before making the choice to pursue what you truly desire and deserve. You don't have to face extreme hardship to make a change. Right here, right now, you can wake up and open your eyes to your unlimited potential and opportunities.

Your life path has to start with you, and if you're unclear about your journey, that unclearness will reflect in your life experiences. You will be shown situations where everything seems to be so puzzling and difficult. However, when you become clear and have a firm definition of what you want your life to look like then that also will show up in your experiences. Decide to have that clarity in you by setting an intention of what you want to experience in this life and who you want to become. If your life is still blurry to you at this moment, then maybe you haven't really looked into it through 20/20 vision. Sometimes we need to disconnect from the world in order to connect with ourselves. Make time to self-reflect and truly envision your life through your lens. Maybe reading this book is a sign for you to make that decision. It's never too late to learn more about yourself, and it's never too late to plan the life you want.

The Life You Desire

What are the experiences in this life that you want to have? To answer this question, make a list. You'll be surprised at how many wonderful things are out there waiting for you! The good thing about the questions I throw at you in this book is that just because they are designed to help you in this very moment, that doesn't mean that your answers need to be set in stone for life. You will always transform, and your desires in life will keep changing according to your growth and circumstances—and that is okay. When you evolve, your standards go along with your transformation. The wiser you become, the richer your desired experiences. So nothing is fixed right now, everything is going to move. For now, the important thing is to identify what you want in this very moment. There is a sense of belongingness once you identify your path and desired experiences. This is how you begin to create your reality; it represents you marking the starting point and going with the flow of life that's right for you according to what you want.

My Struggle with Clarity

I was working as a call center agent for almost five years, and during that time I never had a clear vision of what I truly wanted in life. I was just reporting to work to get paid so I could spend my earnings. However, I did have several short-term goals, such as saving up for travel expenses, buying things I needed, and keeping myself fed. Then I began to watch my closest friends from work move forward and leave the company. As I observed each of them moving on, I asked myself how they did that when there were greater advancement opportunities working for that company since they'd been there for a while. I then realized they decided to leave because they had other plans for their lives. Then and there I saw I needed to decide what I really wanted in the long run. I needed to have my own plan! Since I never saw myself working as a call center agent for the long-term, I had to decide where to go next. After reflecting on this for some time, I realized I wanted a job that offers me flexibility. I wanted to work without going to an office. It wasn't even one of those "big" goals people set for themselves; I was just trying to find something that would provide comfort at that time. From that decision, I quit my job, bought a new laptop, and looked for a home-based job. Two weeks after leaving my job at the call center, I was hired to work from home. I got what I wanted because I identified what it was, I took action, and—most importantly—I believed that it would happen. There are plenty of things I want to experience, and I have more confidence in manifesting them into my reality because I know myself better; therefore, I have a clearer vision of everything that I want in life. The clearer it is to me, the higher chances of it happening for me.

When you have a picture of how the future looks and it's nowhere close to present reality, don't discount your present moment. There is a reason why you are where you are right now, so appreciate it and enjoy it. As for those years I spent

CHAPTER 2: PLANNING THE LIFE YOU WANT

in the call center, I thoroughly enjoyed my time and learned so much from work and from the people around me. The friends I met from that job are still a part of my life, and we have remained good friends.

Your present circumstance eventually makes sense in the future. So hold your present moment with kindness and set an intention to gain clarity about how your path will unfold and start from there.

Envision Your Best Version

There is a shortcut to deciding what your path looks like, it's peeking into a reality that doesn't seem to exist at this moment, but is something you want to make real. One thing that has been working so well for me is envisioning the best version of myself. When you do this, it creates a roadmap for you to get started. So how do you see yourself as your "best version"? When I do this, I see myself as someone who doesn't have limiting beliefs and is courageous enough to explore experiences that offer incredible wisdom. Because it's my wish to become this person, I'm slowly learning how to embody it. If you keep telling yourself that you're not good enough, then you're only going to be exploring the reality of that idea. It's understandable to feel this way, since the society we live in has exposed us to comparison since we were young. People would always root for the successful ones, and that creates the illusion that we aren't as good as those who already have proven themselves.

Going Within

You can break that way of thinking. I want to see myself believing in my own abilities without considering the usual standards of society. I want my confidence to come from my inner self and not from outside validation. My best version would be someone who chooses to move forward to enjoy life and to gain more wisdom—at the same time, to have equal respect and admiration for those people who made it own their own. How about you? How do you picture your best version? Answer this and make an unlimited list of who you want to be.

If you have a hard time deciding your path, imagine you're being granted three wishes right now. What are your wishes? Your wishes are most likely what you truly desire in life in this moment. Write those down and remember to believe that anything can happen for you. This is your life and you got this.

Taking Inventory

Sometimes asking lots of questions can help get you to a clearer vision of your desired path.

- What are the things that you like doing at this moment?
- What are the things that ignite creativity in you?
- What are the things that you want to experience, and what is the path you want compared to what you have right now?

CHAPTER 2: PLANNING THE LIFE YOU WANT

- What kind of person are you to yourself and to others?
- What are the things you like about yourself and what are the things you want to change?

With better clarity around your path, you can work in a direction to get there. Sometimes, it means dropping habits that no longer serve you. For example, if you want to become a yoga teacher, but you'd rather watch TV than do the training it takes to become one, you're out of alignment with your path. If you want to become good at what you do, you have to focus on learning and changing your routines to prioritize becoming better at it. It takes action and a lot of follow-through to get to where you want to go (but it's going to be worth it).

The most important thing now is to learn to focus on the good . Forget about any negative self-talk, shed your worries,and forget about your fear of failure. You don't need to hold onto the things that weigh you down—only take what lifts you up! Do yourself a favor and learn to let these things go.

Going back to Chapter One, focus on the idea of identifying yourself with the goodness the world can offer. When you learn/accept to see your true nature in the light of being happy (high-vibe, in the flow of love)—rather than in the absence of it—it's easier for you to notice what you need to let go of and what you need to hold onto. Your feelings toward what you're going through are already a good indicator of whether you should let go or hold on. But to help you more, here are a few questions to ask yourself:

- Is this situation/person/path giving me joy?
- What value do I get from this situation/relationship/path?
- Is this situation/person/path supportive of my growth?
- What is the reason I should continue with this versus the reason I shouldn't?
- Is this feeling/situation/person/path in alignment with my values?

The Role of Gratitude

There is a misconception that when you want something more or something else, that you are ungrateful for what you have. That's not always the case—you are always going to be drawn to experiences that will help you learn more. After all, you are meant to explore to see your unlimited potential and opportunities unfold! However, it's very important to also appreciate what you have right now. Remember to remain appreciative even to your smaller wins. Being grateful is fuel to achieve greater heights. When you are ungrateful, your reality brings experiences that reflect that ungratefulness. On the flip side, when you are grateful and present you learn to accept that change is necessary in order to grow—and your reality will show you the same idea.

Most of the time, we're so used to living a life doing things routinely to the point that we operate automatically. We get up in the morning, we eat, we drink coffee, we go to work. These repetitive actions put us into auto-pilot mode, in which we forgo mindfulness in favor of the familiar. When your mind isn't present, you miss the little details and those include your small everyday wins. When you at least pause for a minute or two to focus on being grateful, you will be able to analyze your life accordingly and deeply recognize where you want to go and how you're going to get there.

Where Do You Want To Go?

If you don't know where, again, you can always pretend you've been granted three wishes and start from there. Ask yourself, why those wishes? What are your reasons behind them? From here, additional realizations you haven't even thought of before may reveal themselves, and this is where things start to fall into place. I understand how hard it is to imagine that we could achieve what we want when what we are seeing is too far off from our desires. As humans, we tend to focus more on our responsibilities, like the bills we pay. We focus on the tangible reasoning, and in return, we shut down our own possibilities. Just because from a logical standpoint, your goals seem impossible to achieve, that doesn't mean it's not going to be possible. That's why it's important to set your goals and forget about the realities of the world, try to just come up with things you want to achieve, just as a child dares to dream. Dream without inhibitions—just with excitement of what's to come!

Finding My Path

I published this book on my own, so you might think I had a clear vision of my path. But no, I was lost for a while. I did not know what I truly wanted, and I basically was just going with life and where it took me. I was able to enjoy those days of being asleep to my truth; however, at the end of the day, I always felt like something was off. It was like I was functioning like a robot, only doing things for the sake of it without really pondering why. I never truly understood why I was here, but I knew since I was a child that I just wanted to be happy, and I also wanted for my loved ones to feel the same. I used to have the belief that finding your passion was too cliché and the idea only existed because it was hyped so much. Until one day, I remembered back to when I was a child…I always had this thought that there is more to life than what I could see. Because this thought wouldn't leave my mind, I dedicated time to learn more about myself and my purpose in this world.

At first, I desired financial abundance, and so I studied hard to learn about it and how to achieve it. That intention of wanting to become financially free opened so many doors to me. In the process, I learned important things about myself as I deepened my spirituality that have way more value than what money can buy. That passion is real, and it's true what they say. It feels so good to find yourself doing what you love. I wouldn't have experienced these awakenings if I didn't decide to learn something about how to become financially successful. I would have not written this book. Sometimes the initial action you take toward something doesn't end up how you expect it to be; sometimes it's even better than what you sought out to discover. As long as you're open to growth and change, and you know what you want, you will be surprised by what you uncover. After being awakened to my purpose in this life, I realized that my decisions in the present impact my future. So I made sure that my actions now are well thought-through because one way or another it will affect how my future looks. Either way, I'm happy I found a spot for myself now, and I'm excited for what's to come.

How about you...

- Where do you go from here?
- What are your plans?
- What are the things you want to experience?
- What kind of relationships do you want to have?
- What are the things you want to achieve?

Start plotting your story, it's definitely going to get better once you decide to step up.

Start Living Your Dream Life

Everything starts with a decision. Today, tell yourself you are going to start living your dream life. Your dream life is just one decision away from where you are right now. It could be anything you want and dream of, as long as you believe you're worthy of having that kind of life and if you are willing to be open to changes that will come along your way to help you get there.

If you look back, you'll realize that even when you were young, life taught you so many lessons. By observing your life in the present and comparing it to how your childhood days went, you can definitely tell from your experiences as a child what you want in life now. Your parents or guardians might have taught you how to live your life accordingly, but you're now accountable for your own life, and you get to choose. Not everyone has that freedom, so you should embrace it and make the most out of it.

If we don't make decisions for ourselves, others are going to step in to do it for us. If that happens, it's going to be difficult to navigate to a path when we have someone else driving our lives. Imagine being chauffeured to your destination; yes, it is comfortable, and you are always at ease. But as a passenger, your main focus will be the destination. In other words, you are only interested in the outcome and not the journey itself. But remember, the end goal is not all there is; the reason goals become satisfying when achieved is not because they have been reached, but because the drive to get there was fun. If you want to fight for something, fight for the things you want in life. Your inner self is calling you to be courageous for others and mainly for you. Step into your power and mark

CHAPTER 2: PLANNING THE LIFE YOU WANT

your own legacy by deciding to start. If you're already living it right now, then give yourself a big hug for choosing you and for always looking after your inner desires. You have just proven to yourself that you have a say in your life which makes sense since this is your life, this is your experience. But also take note that we're meant to grow, so keep your doors open for even better adventures to come along in your journey. Always remember to take accountability for your own life by deciding to live it on your own terms and in accordance with your heart.

CHAPTER 3

Relationships

CREATING YOUR HARMONIOUS WEB

Relationships are something you should consider when it comes to planning the life you want. We are not alone in this journey; we have other people surrounding us. It only makes sense to identify the kind of relationships you expect to have in your life. Even though we each have our own identity, relationships can still influence our beliefs, actions, and outlook on life. It is better to find alignment in every form of relationship you have, because there is comfort and belongingness in finding healthy relationships. In this chapter, we'll delve into how to create healthy relationships.

What are you looking for in a relationship? What are your expectations with your relationships? Once you have these identified, you will never find yourself swallowed up by a relationship. You will also have a certain standard that you've set for yourself—you don't just let people come into your life, because you will have established healthy boundaries. You will discover the importance of your well-being and how it's better to be around people with whom you feel aligned. Also, you will never be that person who begs for someone to be in your life because you understand healthy relationships are not forced; they are natural. If you can figure out the kind of relationship you want to grow, logically, you will never let yourself be involved in something you don't want and is not right for you.

One of our weaknesses as individuals is when we get too attached to someone else or to anything outside of us. It's something that we can't avoid as we are living in a place where we are surrounded by people. First, we belong to a family; and secondly, we are a part of the community. The older you get the more you accumulate friends and acquaintances; that is, unless you've chosen a different way of life, perhaps off the grid in the woods, abandoning the usual, community-based lifestyle. However, even if you decide to be alone you likely still identify yourself with people who are part of your life, such as your family, parents, closest friends, spouse—and even pets. You are always expected to have someone associated with you, whether a biological or social connection. The reason I've dedicated an entire chapter to relationships is that some people make relationships feel and look too complicated, when they can be simple and thoroughly natural. I believe learning how to have healthy relationships should be taught to everyone, starting at a young age, because it's an important part of our human experience.

Healthy Relationships as a Web

The most natural example I can compare with relationships is a spider on its cobweb. If you see a spiderweb, notice the intricate nature of the web's strands and how perfectly they are aligned. Metaphorically, those web strands represent our relationships, and we are the spider sitting in the middle of it all. From a perspective of a spider, the webs are needed to secure a spot to rest; they have to be strong and dependable. At the very beginning, the spider likely already knows what it wants to build before it takes action. I'm sure the spider is fully aware of its own capabilities when it comes to producing those silk cobwebs in order to build what it can call home. When your relationships are perfectly aligned to you, they become a good source of support for your journey in this lifetime. Individually, you are the spider in your story; at the same time, you represent one of the cobweb's strands that supports someone else's life. By playing that role, you create harmony and a feeling of belongingness for your loved ones.

As easy as it sounds, things don't always simply fall into place. Life is full of experiences that we grasp onto, to the point that we get attached to them as part of how we identify ourselves. We hold onto those things and people who keep us sane and make us feel comforted, but we also unconsciously hold onto those that aren't good for our well-being. A strong strand of web alone is enough to serve as a foundation for the ideal cobweb we're trying to create. But sometimes we don't have enough faith in others or ourselves, so we end up accumulating multiple strands that aren't compatible just to convince ourselves we are doing alright. Sadly, this is how some function in life and especially with relationships. Yes, you are living a life in which you experience things to learn and grow. But you need to recognize when it makes sense to remove yourself from hollow relationships.

Meditation and learning to become mindful of your thoughts can help you identify which connections no longer serve you and can empower you to let them go. The more you connect with the light within, the easier it will be for you to see the difference between what you want and deserve, as well as what your emotions want you to feel in any given moment (such as during a breakup, or conflicts with family, or a rough patch with a friend). You'll discover there is no point in continuously holding on to experiences and people who don't make you feel inspired or at peace. What's the point of being miserable in life, in your relationships? If you begin with introspection, you will be able to figure out the rest of the things outside of yourself. Self-awareness helps you get clear on what you want in a relationship, what you deserve, and how you should show up in order to keep strong alignment with your loved ones. Just like the spider, you'll build a beautiful and intricate web that withstands time and seasons.

CHAPTER 3: RELATIONSHIPS

No Attachments

Continuing with the spider analogy... Have you noticed how the spider doesn't care if the web is broken the next day? They don't get attached to the web they created, for they know how to recreate it over and over. A spider can choose to only have one strand of web or have a big wide web where it settles in for awhile, in which it feels aligned and sits in the middle of everything. Nature shows us that we are the spider, and our relationships are the web. How do you think the spider creates webs so aligned and beautiful? They know what they want, and they know how to do it. They understand they have everything within them to create another one, if not a replica of the previous web, they can make another one that's even stronger and more intricate. And notice when it rains, the spider doesn't fret. The spider is confident enough that instead of worrying, they start strategizing about how to build a new one that suits the current weather. As such, imagine your life as the spider and create your relationship cobweb so it's perfectly aligned with your inner truth. Not because you can, but because that is what you deserve.

When a person starts a relationship with you, they don't create the web for you. You let them become a part of it. And if that person leaves, it's not like you're left with nothing. Always remember: you are the spider, you produce your own web, and you can rebuild it any time!

Relationship With Yourself

This isn't also just about your relationship with other people, this is about your relationship with yourself. As discussed in Chapter One, everything starts within you. If you have a good relationship with yourself, your environment will project what you have inside you. Imagine your life as a road map, you mark specific points as your starting point toward your life path, career path, and relationships. It's simply identifying the good things you want to have in each area of your life, and in this case, you identify the road map you want for your relationships. On this specific road, it's normal to find a stop sign as an indication for you to pause and assess things that are going on around your relationships with other people. Here you will figure out what is working and what isn't. You will analyze your relationships (it may be your relationship with yourself or your loved ones) and take time to fully recognize what's best for you and for the relationship, and see how to move forward with the same clarity until you encounter the next stop sign. There's nothing wrong with making mistakes and finding yourself in the middle of nowhere broken from a heartbreak because that is what the stop sign is for, to learn, to reflect and to find courage to carry on.

Others' View of Your Relationships

It's so common for us to judge our relationships according to someone else's perspective. You can't believe your relationship is ideal or healthy only based on others' opinions or based on how your favorite movie or book portrays love. There is nothing wrong with others offering opinions; the only thing that can go wrong is if you base your judgment on those opinions as opposed to trusting in your own perspective.

For example, someone else may see your relationship with your spouse as healthy—or the opposite of it. However, as the person inside the relationship, you don't necessarily have the same view because you are experiencing it. Outsiders will only have a limited view; you will have the better understanding.

The way our society is oriented, getting influenced by what others say is inevitable, especially when it comes to family and friends. If you establish a strong connection with yourself, you can trust your judgment is purely yours. You can respect others' perspectives, but you can also filter out that which doesn't resonate or align with your values. You are special and unique on your own—there is something about you that nobody has. If you live a life under the influence of others, you silence your voice, your worth, and your abilities.

Going Within

Here are some ways to assess your relationships using your own judgment. To discern if a person is good or bad for you, always go back to how secure you are in your identity. To know how it feels to be in a good relationship, you have to have that good relationship within yourself first. When you are loving toward yourself, you'll feel how love works. When you are treating yourself well, you will know how to treat others the same way. If others don't respect you the way you respect yourself, then they are not your people. With self-awareness, you will be able to set a standard for a healthy relationship, and the basis for this isn't found in other people's stories, it is found in the relationship you have within you. As you work toward cultivating this relationship with yourself, here are some questions to consider:

- Do you treat yourself with kindness?
- Do you root for yourself?
- Do you believe in your abilities?
- Are you patient with yourself?

It's easy to lose yourself when you become so focused on the people around you. But your life is only a projection of what's inside of you. You can't fix anything from the outside, if what's broken is inside. Appreciate your wins and celebrate your everyday effort to live more authentically. Every day, you make decisions that may or may not support your well- being. Don't forget to give yourself credit for the ones that succeeded or for the ones that failed but you learned from. Let go of the idea that selflove is selfish; the only selfish thing is when you depend on someone's love because you think you are incapable of showering yourself with that kind of love. Loving yourself is one of the greatest gifts you can give to the people around you, not only does it reinforce your value, it also doesn't cost you anything. Take time to appreciate yourself because you deserve all the praise in the world! You are here, living life, learning life, and at the same time navigating toward your desired path. Commend yourself for being in the driver's seat, for seeking adventures, and always holding on to the good side of things even when the road gets bumpy.

Family Relationships

Relationships start at home. Not all of us get to be born in a family that has a good environment. Some have broken families, or some have emotionally abusive relationships growing up. If you have not built a strong foundation within yourself at this point of your life, there is a high chance that you are still blaming your misery or hopelessness in your circumstances both in the present and in the past, maybe pointing your finger to your parents or to your siblings and relatives. But if you have learned to take accountability for how your life should be in the present despite how it looked like in the past, you will broaden your understanding of life. You will be more accepting of things that already happened—whether good or bad—and realize that they happened for a reason. You don't dwell on things that did not work; instead, you place your focus on the things that could work. You have a deeper understanding that there are things outside of you that you can't change or control, and that is okay.

Do you know the saying that if you want to marry a guy find someone like your dad? This wasn't how I felt because I didn't approve of my dad. I used to imagine how much better our lives would have been if he was more financially responsible.

As I matured, I realized that he's not perfect (nobody is) and I shouldn't see only his flaws, but also remember his goodness and his compassionate nature. It's true we can't pick our biological family, and it's inevitable that some families don't get along. It's nothing new. We're born with differences, and sometimes it's hard to find harmony, especially if we keep entertaining the noise and the standards of society instead of looking inward. Consider this:

- What kind of relationship do you want to have in your family?
- What kind of relationship do you want to build in your home?

Identifying what you want will help you get your expectations met in relationships. You may not be able to change others, but you can treat them as you want to be treated. When they notice you being open-minded, trusting, loving, and caring to them, those who resonate with you will eventually mirror that behavior. When they see you projecting nothing but good, they will show you the same kind of energy. This may not work in all cases, but at least you're focused on what you can do and what you want rather than what you can't change. When you want for someone to treat you in ways you like, it's better to give them that treatment rather than to ask them for it. Unfortunately, there will be people who are not going to mirror you, and this is how you will know that these people are not in alignment with you.

CHAPTER 3: RELATIONSHIPS

And just because you are blood-related, it does not mean you have to try hard to get along with those who are not resonating with you. It's easier to let go of the attachments you have with these kinds of people when you acknowledge that they are not against you, they are just not aligned to you. When you start treating people according to how their energy resonates, you let go of the belief that you have to work things out because you are related. Being related is not an excuse for any abuse. Being related doesn't have to hold you back from expressing who you want to be. If your sibling or parents don't understand your perspectives, it doesn't mean that they are putting you down; it only means that they are not on the same wavelength as you. Also, if they are not there yet, it doesn't mean they will never get there. So be patient if your family doesn't support you or understand you. Don't take it personally, what others show you is not because of how you are to them, it's how they are inside of themselves.

Family is important. We all have stories of our families; each are unique but similar at one point. Growing up you might not have been able to identify things, but when you look back you will realize how much your experiences as a child shaped who you are today. I wish we all got to experience a supportive and happy family life, but given that people usually get married for all the wrong reasons, it's understandable when things fall apart. This is why it's important to understand yourself; when you do, you can understand others better. Know that even though you are tied to one another, each of the members of your family has their own individuality they need to nurture. Your life is not someone else's responsibility. When you learn not to cling to people so much, you leave them with enough for them to nurture themselves. Your family is a projection of your parents' relationship with each other and their individual relationships with themselves. Just because they are your parents doesn't mean that they are healed from their wounds, it doesn't mean that they don't have issues. As a child, you don't usually notice the things going on around you growing up, but when you reach that point in life when you can identify things, you will understand the complexity of it—and see how simple it should be.

Regardless of your family upbringing, always remember that your past doesn't have to define you. Anytime you decide to move beyond bad experiences in your life, you can. Of course, this is not a book on how to fix family issues, but a book about how to be in a relationship with yourself and project that into your relationships now and in the future. Imagine a household full of individuals awakened to their own truth and loving themselves. The house becomes a home, and differences are complementary rather than destructive. When you wake up to a family with members who willingly take care of themselves, take accountability for their lives, respect others, and love themselves for who they are, you wake up into a family that is loving and manifesting in harmony with you. If your mother is happy and doing what she loves, she will project that into the home. If your father is not stressed out from his day-to-day job to provide for the family or not anxious about gaining outside validation, most likely he will be a better father. If your sibling is content and motivated to follow his or her dreams, then most likely he or she is going to be a supportive sibling to you. Even if you're related, no one should expect someone who is empty to support someone else. This is literally about filling your own cup first so you can be a better parent, son, daughter, sister, or brother. Be aware of what makes you happy, satisfied, and fulfilled and when you reach that contentment, ask your family to do the same for themselves. Not because they need to be aligned to your awareness, but because they deserve to be happy, satisfied, and fulfilled as well!

Romantic Relationships

Romantic relationships are usually portrayed as difficult to find or as taking a lot of effort to work. Changing your mindset toward how you see romantic relationships is the beginning of finding the right person for you. Just shifting the story you tell yourself will bring a different experience. As always, everything goes back to being self-aware. It is the key to identifying the kind of relationship you want to have and the kind of person you want to end up with. Most romantic relationships fall apart because the foundation was not built in the beginning. A strong relationship isn't formed merely out of attraction and spark, although it can start there. It takes a lot of communication to go beyond the surface to really know someone.

Sometimes you get to know people not according to how they treat you—but according to how they treat themselves.

- What kind of relationship do you want to have?
- Who is your ideal partner?
- Why do you want this kind of person to be your partner?

Before you put your standards out into the world, build them up within you first. If you want a secure relationship, make sure you have that security within you, so you don't treat your partner as a security blanket. If you want a trusting partner, make sure you trust yourself, so if someone betrays you, you will still trust your own instincts and guides. Again, everything is a projection of what you have within you.

Honing Discernment by Knowing Yourself

When you feel whole, it's easier to pinpoint what's nourishing in life, and you are not easily blinded by temporary "treats" or fake affections of those who aren't really looking for a partner in life. The truth is some people who enter into relationships are actually just seeking self-validation. Looking beyond what people show you to their true intentions can help you glimpse how the relationship might look like if you were to you pursue this person. It is crucial to learn how to read people and see their genuine intention because it's not only that you are going to work on a relationship with this person, but you will also have a fair share of their energy as a whole. Here are a few pointers for reading people:

- Trust your intuition: If you feel something is off, take some time to observe what it is that is bothering you and why is it bothering you.
- Know their motives: Are they around you because it benefits them (you always do more for them, conditional hangout, they remember you most when they need help, in distress)? Or are they around you because they want a genuine connection (rarely ask for favor, see each other to have fun, remembers you when they're happy)?
- Know what's in the conversation: Is there a give and take or is the conversation just about the other person (all the time)? Do they care what you have to say, or do you feel like you are only in the conversation to receive what they have to say?
- Assess yourself: If you start feeling that you are not good enough around certain people, that's a sign.

When you have self-awareness, you can easily detect people who don't have it. People who are working hard to learn from their mistakes and choosing to get up each time they fall are examples of individuals who have clarity within them. Awakened people are learners, and they walk the talk. They don't depend on others to fix their lives; they are responsible, and they own their decisions. Some people carry too much baggage within them, and if you are part of a relationship in which you feel responsible for fixing things for your partner or helping them carry their own baggage, that is a big red flag. If you are not self-aware, you will see it as being there for someone because you love them, but if you have self-awareness, you will understand that the right person will help themself and try to not burden others, not even their partner.

Life is about our individual experiences—it's about taking accountability for our own circumstances. Relationships don't exist to erase accountability; relationships exist to find harmony despite the differences and to have a healthy support system to inspire you to grow. If someone is turning over their responsibilities like it is yours, how is that a good foundation? If someone is taking advantage of you, playing mind games, and making you feel bad about yourself all the time, how is that a healthy support system? There is nothing wrong about making bad decisions and falling for the wrong person, the only thing that is wrong with it is if you let yourself repeat that same agony over and over again. Remember: pain has value when you learn and grow from it. Being hurt is not necessarily bad when it awakens you to what you truly want to feel. But if you unconsciously put yourself in the same circumstances that deliver you the same results, you will end up feeling depleted.

So how are you going to find the right person? The answer: within you.

CHAPTER 3: RELATIONSHIPS

My Story

My husband, Shane, is from California. Several years ago, he decided to travel to the Philippines by himself as it had always been his dream to visit a tropical country. I met him in a mall around the time I was moving on from a failed relationship, and we were so in alignment about what we wanted in life, everything just clicked.

Before I met him, I did not know what I truly wanted in a romantic relationship. I thought that the people who showed up in my life were just part of the entire story and that I just lived with it because I didn't know I could create my own life and experiences. At that point, this statement was true to me, but now I finally understood that I stumbled upon those relationships which ended because I wasn't being clear about what I truly wanted. But because of those relationships that did not work in the past, it caused me to be at the stop sign of my relationship road map, and I had that time to ponder. When I had that stop, I finally became aware of setting my own standards and only settling for what I want. When you are clear, the Universe will deliver clarity; if you are indecisive, you will be shown confusing experiences. When I finally identified what I wanted at the same time believed that it was possible, I met someone who has all the qualities of a human being I was seeking. Now, I'm married to that person, and all the wrong turns, unexpected stops, well, they were all worth it.

Going Within

If you want a desirable partner, what are the traits you are looking for? Do you have those traits in the first place? Think of a mirror, who you see will be projected into your reality. Your beliefs about people will be the basis of what you recognize in the people around you:

- If you love yourself, you will be shown people in your life who do the same thing.
- If you want a partner who is loving, love yourself. If you want a partner who is giving, treat yourself.
- If you are desperate to find a partner because you don't want to be alone, then the mirror will put you into experiences that will validate your desperation—and you will always be put in situations where you feel desperate.

Finding the right partner is more about an alignment of mind and heart that is somewhat intangible. It's being awakened to your truth that gets you to the people who are aligned to you. What is your truth? Take some time to journal about this. There is a beautiful mystery that occurs during the process of awakening that only you can experience. It's an individual moment that I would never try to paint for someone else. It is delivered in a flow specific to how you are as a person, how you think, feel, and most important, how you love yourself and others.

It's good to have your alone time, but life can feel more fulfilling when you are surrounded by people you care about.

As always, your relationship with yourself is the highest priority. Learn to appreciate your efforts and find time to delve deeper into what you want in your primary relationships.

Healthy Relationships Versus Toxic Relationships

When you are not seeing things from a conscious perspective, you can easily get swayed by how others want you to see things. Then it becomes hard for you to tell if a toxic relationship is toxic or not. First, you have to identify what a healthy relationship looks like to you. Second, when you get exposed to a relationship that doesn't feel healthy, just by noticing what is good and bad for you, you will be able to recognize toxicity when you're in it. When you become the observer of your experiences, you can see it in a more neutral point of view. From there, you can observe the experience without being emotionally attached. The thing is, if you are not self-aware, you will never see these things in a perspective of clarity, and it's harder for you to identify which is which.

When it comes to relationships, you will be able to tell if it's not good for you because it will not feel right. If you start to lose touch with yourself to keep the relationship going to the point that you become someone else even in your own eyes, that is a hint that something is off. Relationships will not feel right if love is not present, and that environment breeds toxicity.

A toxic relationship is when someone asks more of you than what you can give—or have already given. It's a constant feeling of trying to do the work to keep everyone happy to maintain the relationship. It's a constant feeling of not being good enough so you find yourself coming up with something to please or fix things to convince people to stay. A healthy relationship is natural, it doesn't require as much effort; it only requires you to be yourself. It is smooth and easy. It flows naturally without any other requirements but just to be who you are. In a toxic relationship, you are always anxious. You have plenty of "what-if's." But in a healthy relationship, you are confident, happy, and content. You have no need to prove anything, you can just relax into your true self. You are accepted, and your flaws are welcome without judgment.

Of course, in any relationship there will still be compromises since people have differences, that's why communication is important so we can overcome the contrast and meet in the middle. In a toxic setting, communication isn't always open, thinking is one-sided, and beliefs are fixed. But in a healthy relationship, communication is key, growth is desired, and sharing ideas is a wonderful thing.

When you're with the wrong people, you can feel it; you can feel the misalignment. If you catch yourself trying to be someone else in order to fit in, then maybe it's about time for you to evaluate things. Remember that your imperfections are normal, and if you have people around you telling you otherwise, then maybe they are not suited for you at this moment. Toxic relationships are based on what you can do for them, healthy relationships are based on mutual love and respect. And if you feel like you are screwed for being in the wrong relationship, don't worry, because you will learn so many valuable lessons from your experience. Remember, we are here to learn. And if, at some point you feel that you were the toxic one in a relationship, acknowledge it and understand that you needed to go through this in order to witness it in your own eyes and to comprehend it best. That way, you are able to truly identify what feels right to you and how you should move forward as a result of your experience.

CHAPTER 4

Career

A CATALYST TO YOUR PASSION

In this chapter, we'll look at the importance of your chosen career path in terms of providing for your monetary needs. We'll also touch on the values you can derive from your career aside from the mere financial benefit.

Our society is set up in such a way that we are encouraged to choose a career in order to be more "effective" in life. We are drilled on how and why we should enter into a certain job or profession. There seems to be so much conflict around pursuing what lights you up or being practical about your career choice.

In addition, because society is oriented so that we need to bring in money in order to live, many settle for what's available to pay the bills—it's simply always an easier choice for most people. Every time you settle for a job that you despise, that choice hurts your possibilities for manifesting your dream career, because you are signaling to the Universe that you don't believe you can have it—or that you deserve it. I always picture a career change in the direction of your passion like skydiving. At first, it looks terrifying, but the moment you jump off the plane, you realize that it's the most exhilarating experience of your life! Fortunately, nowadays more and more people are motivated to put their focus into doing what they love even if it means they have to give up something and make adjustments (such as giving up a lifestyle that's only possible if you have a fixed income or learning to use your own resources to become fully independent). Of course, there are also those who are content and happy living in the 9-to-5 world, which is a wonderful thing. There are also those who are miserable in their jobs, complain about them, and yet do nothing to change their situations.

Going Within

When you carve out time to reflect on what's important to you, it becomes easier to resolve any issues you're experiencing around your career journey. If you know you are stuck in a job that you don't like, then what are you doing to change it?

- Are you saving money?
- Are you planning to start a business?
- Are you eyeing a new job?
- Are you planning to go back to school to advance your career?

These are the simple questions that you should meditate on if you are not satisfied with where you are on your professional path. If you are not grateful about your current job situation, you need to pause and reflect. Sit with it for some time because if you are bothered by your situation, it requires your attention. After evaluating things, you can start building a plan to get to a place that will fulfill you. One of the main reasons people don't know how—and when—to take action even though they don't like their jobs is they don't know themselves well enough to know where they're headed. They don't love themselves enough to believe that they can make a change; in other words, they don't pay attention to themselves, they are always distracted with everything else. But if you are someone who practices self-awareness, you know what you want and how to get to it. As someone who practices self-awareness, you also prioritize your happiness because you know this is your responsibility.

You gain strength and courage to pursue the things you desire, even if it takes you in a different direction, you feel confident that you can come up with a plan and make things happen.

Challenges Lead to Lessons

It comes down to choosing to grow and doing what your heart desires or settling into your comfort zone because it's familiar. In this life, you will be presented with experiences in which you have to ponder the path to choose for the sake of learning how to choose. Unfortunately, many still don't stop to look at things from a point of view of learning from each experience. Challenges are there to show you the lesson of choosing yourself, and if you don't get it, you will have the same experiences all over again. And you will keep having the same issues—but with different people at different times. The goal is to learn from your experiences. Once you can apply the learning to your life, your new realization will bring about new experiences.

For example, let's say you have been employed at a certain company for a long time but keep getting overlooked for a raise or promotion. Regardless, you decide to stay with the company. Then, someone new starts and shortly thereafter receives a raise and promotion. That may lead you to think the company doesn't like you or you need to do more to prove yourself. This experience is trying to teach you to see your own worth so others will, too. It is teaching you to articulate what you want and act on it. If you feel you deserve a raise (because you're doing a great job) it's on you to understand your worth and open that discussion with your supervisor. If the company dismisses that—even knowing how much value you bring to the company—that's a clear sign to move on and find a new job.

When you can decide what's best for you in this kind of situation it's because you know your worth. But if you don't see your worth, you may blame the company for being biased or cheap or think that you are not good enough and don't care for a raise or promotion as long as the company keeps you (because you think you won't be able to find a new job). And if you move on to a different company but still don't value and believe in yourself, you will experience the same situation. The idea is that your experiences are teaching you a lesson, and if you don't get it the first time, you are going to experience the same circumstances until you understand what it is that you need to take away from it.

Yes, you may get hurt, feel disappointed, and worried. But at the end of the day, you only have one thing to focus on, and that is to get to a place of understanding when it comes to what the experience is trying to teach you. When you get it, you will move forward as things snap into place, just like a puzzle. To keep building the picture of your ideal life, piece by piece, you need to continually go back to your self-awareness and identify your role in your life. Remember: you are the creator of your reality.

Job Versus Passion

I used to tell myself that if there was one thing I could change in this world, I'd want for everyone to quit working if their jobs were only to pay their bills. I'd like for everyone to go out and do something they actually love and not worry about surviving the usual day-to-day life. This is one of the things I desired for myself and for the people around me and the world; however, from my point of view now, wishing for this doesn't make sense anymore, because I understand that we are here to learn. We are here to figure out what we're doing in order to shift into something we truly want.

Sometimes you have to see what you don't want to decide what you do want to experience. It's a very simple idea: You have to be shown what it's like to be sad to realize that it is not what you want to feel. Most of the time, you may think these things are out of our control, but you have influence over them. What you think and feel inside will be reflected in your environment. If you have not decided to identify as someone who is flourishing and optimistic then your reality will reflect that indecisiveness toward your success and being a positive person. In other words, you will be shown experiences that resonate with what you think and feel. If you don't decide what you want to feel and think within, you will be shown experiences filled with vagueness—instead of clarity.

A practical job is as valuable as doing something that truly interests you. It's valuable because it provides you a paycheck so you can live. Accepting that sometimes you have to work to pay for things in life is a good way to process it. It may sound cliché, but it's true that things happen for a reason. Society has created this system as an energy exchange, and since you are here, you need to learn to navigate within it so you can come out better for it, and not the other way around. The outside will always be reflected from what's within you; if you are ungrateful for your current job, you will be shown job opportunities that match the ungratefulness within you—

this may manifest in unpleasant experiences (you get stuck in traffic on the way to an interview, you're offered a low wage, you generally feel like the world is "against" you). And unless you re-examine your thoughts and feelings and decide to become more appreciative for everything you can think of, you will not enjoy the greater opportunities you could have otherwise manifested. A job is a job that you may or may not like especially if it is not something you ever dreamed of doing. But learning to appreciate the value it provides, such as the opportunities, the new skills you accumulate, and new connections you create, will lighten you up. Not only will it provide a monetary value in exchange for your time and energy—it will also help you support your loved ones. Let me explain... If you appreciate what you have, it gives you a warm feeling and contentment inside. The people around you will also be infected by that good feeling within you, which triggers them to do the same because it's contagious! Once you have this appreciative feeling within you, your environment will validate that feeling by putting you into situations that will make you appreciate even more.

Balancing My Job and My Passion

At this moment, I'm really excited to pursue something I love to do— writing. I'm currently only doing it part-time, but sometimes I imagine doing it full-time would make me feel more aligned. I'm currently employed as a customer support representative and work 40 hours per week. It's not that I don't like my job; it's one of my dreams that came true when I decided I wanted the freedom to work from home. My colleagues and the company I work for are wonderful, and there's no reason for me to quit. But sometimes I think of how much more I'd be able to do if I could focus my full attention on doing what I love. Building my craft and truly getting into something that I'm passionate about sounds so dreamy. I can't stop but wonder how it would turn out if I went all in. However, right now, I know I'm still in the beginning stages of the phase I'm venturing into. It's fun to imagine reclaiming my time and spending it on something I'm interested in, but there are other things I need to consider. I have this job for a secure flow of income, and if I don't need to worry about my income then I have access to my creative energy. When I feel anxious about my finances, it's harder to tap into my full creative side. So if I quit my job without taking that into consideration, I wouldn't have enough energy to put toward what I love to do. I'd only end up worrying about money.

I used to quit jobs, but with my current job, I decided to persist and make sure I get to experience the best of both worlds. I had to learn this lesson as the same thing happened to me in the past. I once rushed into giving up a job in exchange for something I thought required my full attention but, in the end, I just came back looking for work so I could pay the bills. The lesson for me now is to be wiser and less abrupt in my decision-making, especially when it involves finances.

As a spiritual person, I trust that I can drop anything that gets in the way of my desires and I will still be okay. However, my current job is not stopping me from pursuing what I love. Instead, I learned that I need to practice better time management in order to balance both. I couldn't touch the 40 hours per week as that is dedicated to my employer. But I needed to drop the unnecessary things in my free time (excessive social media scrolling, binge-watching TV, etc.) that are not necessary and focus instead on my writing. I started going to bed early and getting up earlier to get things done. During the pandemic, like many others, I was home more during the weekends, so I had more time to write. (Even without Covid restrictions, I'd have chosen to stay home more to focus on my passion.) When I realized I only need to practice better time management, the idea of quitting my day job was no longer an option. I also learned that the quickest and easiest decision you can make, isn't always the right one. Perseverance is crucial. What is meant for us happens for us, but in the meantime, we can continue to take action and get something out of the situation, such as identifying what needs to be done and taking small steps to accomplish even a little each day.

In this very moment, I'm writing at 6 a.m. after getting up at 5 a.m., and by 8 a.m., I will start working until 5 p.m. I made sure I dedicated some time to writing every day. I have a belief that in order to produce great things, you have to put in the hard work as well. This is just my belief, and at first, I wanted to get rid of this idea because I also know that it doesn't have to be that way. But I again realized that it is in the hardest times that we discover what we truly need to learn. I can't deny that sometimes I learn best if it's through the hard way. One day, I'll wake up and feel a deep sense of satisfaction, knowing that you read my book and it resonated with you. Until that day comes, I will continue to put in the effort. Even after that day comes, I will continue to put in the "hard" work and write because it is what I love to do. To me, the simplest definition of passion is doing something for yourself. It is about adding value to you—so you can add value to others.

Learning to Appreciate

I've always noticed that our community influences us to always seek better and better opportunities. There's nothing wrong with being ambitious, enjoying life's possibilities, and improving your life for the better. But sometimes, because of the intention to keep reaching for the stars, you may forget to appreciate what you already have. There's a tendency to look ahead and forget how far you've come, to the point that you forget to reflect and realize how much you've already accomplished! If you look back over your life from the perspective of someone who appreciates the present moment, you will gain a better understanding of where you are. The constant desire for something better is positive since you are meant to grow; however, it is also making you chase what you want and focus on what you lack. There's nothing wrong about wanting a better life and experiences as long as you're not forgetting the valuable things you already have in the present moment. The appreciation toward what you've accomplished and the dreams you've reached helps you stay grounded. Some people forget about this phase especially when they know they can get what they want. But please understand that the more you are grateful for what you have, the more you get to where you want to be. And so if there's something you want, appreciate what you already have. There's a reason why you're in a specific situation right now, and one possibility is that it could be a valuable steppingstone toward a new reality. Embrace it!

Appreciating Work

Not too long ago, I had four days off from work, and during that time I couldn't go anywhere because of the lockdown. I ended up staying home for four days. I noticed how I lost track of my time. I slept late from watching random videos on the internet well into the night. I knew I had writing to do, but I was lax about it because my schedule was so wide open. After my time off was up, I saw that I had needed to rest my mind and decided not to beat myself up for being unproductive; instead, I chose to show myself compassion and accept what was.

However, this experience showed me how valuable my current job is in helping me stay consistent with time management and productivity—the structure it provides has kept me on-track with my passion project. If it's a workday, I get up early and make sure to complete my priorities for the day. Reporting to work has made me aware of how I should track my time better and how I can become more productive. Now I have more appreciation for my work, as it not only provides for me financially, but it comes with this added value as well. My job helps me be more organized, which makes me think I might not be equipped to do my own thing at the moment because I lacked the discipline to do it when a stretch of time presented itself, but that's not a judgment; it's just another lesson I can ponder.

An Exercise in Being Present

Appreciation and being in the moment go hand-in-hand because you can't truly appreciate something if you are not giving it your full attention. We often hear people nowadays talking about being present, but what does it truly mean? Here's an exercise to help you experience it for yourself.

Try being in the moment when you wash your hands. This is the simplest way to observe your mind and indulge your senses. When you wash your hands, focus on how it feels when the water touches your palms. Become so present that all you think about is the feeling of the cold water hitting your hands and all you can hear is the sound of the water running from the faucet. Focus only on what you are feeling in the moment. Resist the urge to think about the next steps of grabbing the soap, turning off the faucet, or toweling your hands dry. Just remain there feeling and observing the moment.

That is what being present looks like. It's when you can place your full attention in the moment without entertaining any outside noise. You can practice it during a simple action such as washing your hands or while meditating—it's really up to you and how you feel. If mastered, being present shows you how to be more appreciative of the simple things in life.

Finding Inspiration

No matter how few activities you partake in on a daily basis, inspiration is available. There is inspiration in every day and every action you take—when you choose to notice it all around you. Once you practice being present, it becomes easier for you to find inspiration. At some point, it can be subjective. Some people are inspired only according to how they feel and how they can relate to it. But because of the natural flow of love within you, you are easily inspired by anything that has love in it. It's an innate reaction that produces a wonderful warm feeling within you every time you witness any action inspired by love. The goodness in you is ingrained in your being; however, due to struggles in life you slowly disidentify yourself from that light. Everything exists—good and bad—but what is empowering is your ability to allow what you want to exist in your reality. If you focus on the good, bad can still exist. Negativity does not disappear when you focus on positivity, but it can slowly become unnoticeable to you. When you choose good as your default lens, what you see in the world is to your advantage. This is because "good" is more aligned with wonderful experiences such as unconditional love, abundance, a healthy mindset, serenity, contentment, freedom etc. While bad can still exist, what you focus on is more important, and this is why being present is needed to maintain a good outlook. Not only so you can become conscious of what is happening all around you (especially in the small moments), but so things also become clearer to you, like finding inspiration. It is finding light and hope in the dark. It is choosing the tiny bit of positivity over the enormous heap of negativity.

Once your perspective is focused on finding inspiration versus finding imperfections, your experiences will begin to match what you think and feel. You will see good in the bad, trust in the doubt, and inspiration in the discouragement:

- If you have a job that you're not interested in, you will find inspiration by appreciating the value it gives you.
- You will also understand that every relationship that crosses your path has meaning and letting them go also

has meaning—everything has meaning and in the end it's beneficial for your growth.

Finding inspiration is a combination of being appreciative and being present in the moment. It is noticing the beautiful sun rising in the morning or noticing how the tree dances to the wind, how the birds sing and fly. Or it could be just an ordinary day at home where your cat shares its food with a stray cat. These are inspirations you'd never notice if you don't allow yourself to see them; these are the moments when you appreciate kindness and love beyond words. And these will not be available for you to see unless you allow yourself to be mentally and emotionally present.

Don't forget that one of the greatest inspirations you can find is acknowledging and believing in your own potential! As a result, you become an inspiration to others. And it's not your achievements that people feel inspired by—it's your story. Your life is made up of an accumulation of stories, and what better story to tell than one of living through adversity to see the beauty in everything?

CHAPTER 5

Abundance

RECLAIMING YOUR TRUE WEALTH

In this chapter, we unpack how you view abundance in relation to how it is projected around you and tackle how you can cultivate your own perception of it by recognizing the wealth you already possess. Let me start by asking a question: How important do you think money is in your life? To me, it is very important, and our individual experiences can attest to that. Money is what you use to buy your basic needs and what you use in exchange for something that adds value to your way of life. When you hear the word abundance, what comes to mind? Honestly, I used to believe that abundance had to do with how much money someone had in the bank. I also used to think that when someone was rich, they had power over others who had less. This is how abundance seemed to be portrayed and projected into the society all around me. But as I grew older, I started seeing the broader perspective of abundance and its real value versus how it is presented to us. Yes, money is fundamental, but it isn't just for one reason; there's so much more to it than just the material value it provides. It can provide a good feeling toward your experiences. Money allows you worry less and gives you more freedom to act on your desires.

You can't blame someone who thinks winning the lottery will solve all of their problems. Again, society leads us to believe that money is so important that it's the solution to everything. And while money can for sure help, you can't put it on a pedestal thinking that accumulating plenty of it is the answer to your problems—or it is all that life is about. If you do, you need to re-examine your beliefs about money.

Wealth as a Mindset

There is plenty of wealth in the world that you may fail to acknowledge. Take your existence, for example. If you are here, living, breathing, and experiencing this life, you are already abundant! Wealth represents the abundance of something in your life, and it is not limited to the amount of money you have in the bank. If someone is born into a poor family, you may understand them to be poor because they have so little money and pity them for their status. But even if they lack an abundance of money, their family could be wealthy in other areas such as healthy relationships, genuine love, and happiness. Conversely, there are those who are born

CHAPTER 5 : ABUNDANCE

into wealthy families with plenty of material possessions, but that may be the only form of wealth they believe they have.

Your beliefs toward abundance and wealth don't have to be aligned with how most people in our society view it. I encourage you to look at it through a different lens—having the freedom to choose how you perceive things is another form of abundance. You have free will to see things from your own point of view; you don't have to rely on what is already established and what you've been taught to believe. As long as you can think for yourself and take accountability for your beliefs, there should not be any problems identifying your own treasure.

It's clear that standards that were built years ago and what worked in the past don't necessarily work today. Or what people believed worked for many does not work for everyone. This is why, for example, people living off grid may appear to lead a more content and carefree life than those in a city or suburb, because they chose to live according to how they wanted as opposed to society's standards.

When you detach yourself from the usual standards of society, you free yourself from society's expectations. You free yourself from being tied to achieving something you did not set out to achieve for yourself. There is nothing wrong with being successful in a career or acquiring all the material possessions you want; that is good as long as it is your personal goal. But if you're only living a certain lifestyle for others to see and to fit in or gain acceptance, you may want to re-think your reasoning.

The same thing goes for your definition of wealth; it is subjective and varies from person to person. But most people are only aware of the kind of wealth they were taught to believe in. You may not even notice how you accumulate beliefs that aren't true to yourself, but because of that, you unconsciously follow them because you think it's "the way things should be." It's worth learning to set your own standards of how wealthy you are according to your own perspective and not fall into believing that you should be a certain way for reasons outside of you.

The beliefs you hold onto with money can be scary, since at some point you likely considered it the answer to everything. However, money is just a tool for you to live according to how the physical world exchanges energy. You have to start thinking about what money can do for you, not just in the material aspect, but in reasons beyond that. Let's learn to focus on the feeling money can help you experience, rather than the tangible material it can provide. For example, money can be used to help other people, and helping other people feels good. Money can let you travel and see the world, and exploring places gives you so much freedom and exposes you to different perspectives. Money can get you a new house, a new car, and a comfortable lifestyle. In other words, it can offer you a life with less stress, more carefree experiences, and the result is that it makes you feel appreciative for your life and what you have.

Some people look at money differently; they think being rich is being better than everyone, doing things poor people can't, and buying things others can't afford. Some look at being abundant as a status symbol that separates them from ordinary people, making them feel special by being on top; whereas a humble way of living that provides joy, comfort, and the opportunity to help others is a legitimate form of abundance. When you look at being rich from a perspective of greed, then even if your bank account is bulging, your life will remain empty, because greed is based on lack and fear (we'll get into this idea soon). Real wealthy people not only have enough money for themselves, but they appreciate life experiences and are always curious to learn more, discover, and grow. There is already abundance within us and what surrounds us, we only need to learn to recognize it. I truly believe money will come to those who recognize they are wealthy in other ways (even if it's not yet reflected in their bank account).

Understanding the Value of Money

Some people feel as if money is the root of all evil, whereas others think it's a tool for living a fulfilling life. There is nothing wrong whatsoever in the different ways people view the value of money. The only important thing to remember is that you don't have to be on the same page as everyone else;

you can have your own perception about the value of money, while still respecting others' view of it.

When you perceive money according to how most people see it, then you become like most of those people. You become what you believe in. If you believe money is evil, then money is harder to manifest into your life since most likely you don't want to associate yourself with evil. But if you see money in a different light, you open your eyes to the idea that you can believe in what you want to believe in. You get to create your perception of money, and as mentioned in Chapter One, the important thing is crafting your beliefs in favor of yourself and in the light of goodness. Make sure you believe in something that will elevate your way of living and existence and not the other way around. Continuing with the example of thinking money is evil, if that's your belief, you wouldn't want to acquire as much or even have money, so that could result in you having issues with financial responsibility. However, in an example where you view money as a tool to experience a carefree life, freedom to do what you want, and being able to help others could result in your manifesting lots of abundance to create these positive outcomes. It's empowering to know you have free will to choose how you perceive money—the choice is always yours.

Everything is about how you perceive things. So, try to see money in the eyes of excitement, joy, and love. If you have plenty of money, you have more freedom to do things you want to do without so much blockage—if you feel like you want to travel now, you can! Money is a tool that can provide freedom and ease, allowing you to get the things you want and need. It can also be a source of help to others, not only by supporting causes that are important to you, but by providing an example that lets others see their potential to build their own wealth. If you have plenty of money, you get to eat your favorite expensive dish, travel to your dream destination, remodel your home, and experience other things that help bring about good feelings. Acquiring money offers a lot of opportunities to live your life in this physical world more fully. However, don't forget that you don't want to depend on money for your happiness alone. Happiness needs to come from within you, and having the ability to acquire wealth is just another treat.

Sometimes I compare money to someone's makeup kit. You already know the person is naturally beautiful, but with makeup, it enhances the beauty. Money is like that; it is just a tool. You are naturally rich with love and kindness as they are innate within you, but money can help you enhance those traits. Deep within, you are already rich and have always been since you are made of love and love is an abundance beyond comparison.

Types of Abundance

Now that we've cleared up the idea that money doesn't encompass all of our riches, let's talk about real abundance in life, of which there are many examples, but we'll focus on a few.

The Abundance of Life

You exist with a body that works for you on a planet full of natural resources. It is true when they say that health is wealth; just notice how your body works, it is a brilliant creation! If you look in the mirror and closely look into your eyes, and you'll see how magnificent they are. For a minute, pause and consider that you are fully equipped with the mechanics necessary to live; everything you need is already intact in your body. Think about the amazing way that your mind and heart work. There's no need to get into details, but you already understand that your body is a priceless work of art and you need to take care of it as one of your most precious forms of wealth. There are many reasons to feel gratitude, and existing in this world with a healthy physical body should be one of them.

The Abundance of Relationships

Another abundance you may tend to take for granted is having healthy and genuine relationships. You can't buy a true friend or a good spouse. (I guess you could to some extent, but it wouldn't last long.) Having people around who resonate with you and bring comfort, support, and compassion is special. And what about your good relationship with yourself? That richness deserves your gratitude. When you love yourself, you believe in yourself and your potential. You can achieve whatever you want in life as long as you have faith in yourself. Your security within yourself and your ability to spread positivity will inspire others in your circle and motivate them to find that relationship within themselves. Now isn't that pure gold?

The Abundance of Your Experience and Knowledge

How about your experiences? Whether your life sucked at some point, but you are still here, you have the opportunity to make new memories. You can create experiences that are simple and true to you. How about knowledge? If you know a lot of things and that helps you avoid making bad decisions, that is a form of wealth. And if you are not as wise as you wish and have been making poor decisions—but still you can identify and learn to improve next time, then you are wealthy in that aspect of learning. There is plenty of abundance all around us that we fail to identify because we only focus on what has been shown to us. If you can learn to disidentify yourself from the rules of society or the beliefs of other people, you will be rich in your own ways.

The Abundance of Nature

How about nature? The next time you're outside, look up and take in the vastness of the sky, another piece of proof that you are limitless. If you pay attention to it closely, you'll also see that the ocean represents pure abundance. How can you miss the beauty of it all—the water, the air, the land, and the fire. These are magnificent creations, and if you become more present to appreciate them, you become even more abundant. Money is just a small part of your wealth, so resist the urge to put pressure on it by using it as your whole motivation to live. You are already rich now, and you will always be.

Your life experiences—whether good or bad—are another form of wealth. Nobody else can take them away from you. Think of them as your own resources. You can experience something, and it's up to you to decide how you would capitalize or grow from that experience. Your experiences are unique to you because even if the same things were happening to someone else, you have a different set of senses that allow you to create this filtering system that makes your experiences yours.

Learning how to find abundance in what already exists for you is another ability for which to be thankful. At one point, you might be broke or struggling in the aspect of material possessions, but you have the free will to either focus on what's not happening for you or to focus on what's already available for you. When you feel unworthy and penniless, take comfort in the air you breathe, the sunrises you get to witness, your imaginative mind, and your limitless, compassionate heart. Always remind yourself of the things that are already happening for you that resonate with abundance. You are alive, learning, and experiencing life; pause for a moment and let that sink in.

CHAPTER 5 : ABUNDANCE

Lack Mentality

Lack mentality is about fear—the fear of not having enough. It is not seeing the things you already are abundant in because you only focus on what you lack. Many who have this trait have experienced tough financial issues in the past. Once you start accumulating money, there's an instinct to save more so you don't have the same experience as when you had nothing. Unfortunately, this can lead to more suffering. So, if you want to save money, do it because that is what you want (to have money)—not because you are afraid of losing what you want (not having money). Many people only save with the intention of not losing. In order to feel truly abundant, the feeling needs to be aligned, inside and out.

You see, abundance is not limited to your money and material possession. If you can look at it from this point of view, it will be easier for you to let go of the idea of wanting so you can stop not having. It's healthier to want something for the joy or practical application of it; not because you fear your needs will not be met. When you want something because you genuinely like the idea of having that particular thing or experience, then you are wanting something out of pure intention. But if you want something for other reasons, such as wanting friends so you don't have to feel lonely, is a different story, or wanting money so you don't have to feel broke. If you feel like this, you are not following your heart's desires; you are going after something because of fear of lack.

We all have experienced this at some point in our lives. Lack is truthfully scary, and so you have every right to feel scared. However, if you continuously make decisions in your life based on fear, even if things work out for you, inside you'll still find fear of loss and lack. As always, what's within you and how you feel inside is always going to be projected into your reality. This explains how many rich people—even if they have plenty of money—still continue to have drama and issues in their lives. But there are also wealthy people who have found their truth within themselves and have both material possession and self-care that balances their lives with clarity from within. So they continue to manifest abundance from within and from their awareness of their own beliefs.

Going Within

Sadly, most people still can't discern which beliefs are truly theirs and which are influenced by others. Meditation helps you get into a state where your thoughts are clear. Once you practice being in that clear state of mind, it is easier for you to identify your thought patterns and your beliefs. Once you do, you will also know which beliefs should go and which beliefs you should hold onto. Lack mentality doesn't only apply to acquiring material wealth; it also shows up in other areas of your life.

- If you notice how at some point you wanted to be in a relationship with someone, was it really something

you wanted for yourself or was it born out of feelings of loneliness?
- What about your travels? Did you want to travel for yourself and the joy of the experience, or did you only do it because of FOMO?
- What about your achievements? Did you want them for yourself first, or did you want to reach them to prove to others you could, so they won't think less of you?

It's critical to identify your beliefs so you know which ones have to go to make room for new beliefs that empower you. It can be difficult to see your true intentions from the layers of beliefs that have been put upon you. It can also be difficult to face the fact that at some point you were toxic or at least not living in an authentic way. It's okay to feel this way so you can face your shadows. In order to bring light to the darkness, you have to first identify what is dark and what is light, so you can proceed with clarity through whatever ways you can apply to accomplish your goal of amplifying the light within you.

Since we've tackled how lack mentality can sabotage your potential and opportunities, let's turn to how to shed it. Meditation is always a good first step. Another effective way to clear the fear of lack is to practice gratitude. When you are genuinely grateful, there is no hidden agenda; you are simply thankful for all that you have or experience. Just because you don't have money in the bank doesn't mean there is nothing else to appreciate.

The Power of Gratitude

When you practice being grateful versus being scared of not having, you will create a profound shift in your life and also in how you perceive things. By learning to appreciate the little things in your life (the truth is they're not little; they are big but unnoticed) you create change.

When you practice gratitude, it becomes natural. You become appreciative deep within yourself, and when that happens, your reality shows you more things and experiences for which to be thankful. In turn, you become abundant. You become wealthy not because you are running away from lack, you become wealthy because you are thankful. Having the ability to appreciate despite all the reasons to fear is what makes you naturally, effortlessly rich.

Remember, money is an essential part of your experience in this material world. But it's most important to be grateful for other things that are given less importance by society. It's within your ability to perceive things the way you choose and to only choose beliefs that empower you versus those that limit you. Real wealth lies in believing in your unlimited potential and appreciating opportunities and experiences you already have. Foster your pure excitement over what's ahead of you and live each day with a conscious decision to see gratitude all around you.

CHAPTER 6

Purpose

THE ART OF LIVING CONSCIOUSLY

In this chapter, we'll look at ways you can uncover the profound meaning of your life and learn to live it (practice) in your daily experiences. This is one of my favorite topics, as we are going to delve into the unseen versus the reality we see. Understanding your passion in this lifetime is difficult for some and easy for most—you only need to think of something you enjoy doing and that's it. It could be a creative project you love to work on, or it could be creating experiences for you and for others around you—the sky's the limit! Passion sits within you and you don't need to "find" it, you only need to pause to recognize what you truly love doing. But if you're struggling to find your passion, it is because you are struggling to seeing your purpose. When you are clear on your purpose it's easier to identify your passion. But how do you know your purpose? How do you even learn what it is?

You Are Limitless

If you want to know your purpose, you have to be open to everything, even things that don't appear to be real. When you think about the possibilities outside of your physical life here on earth, you begin to open your mind to greater wisdom. When you choose to only believe in what you already see and what is visible to you at the moment, you are free to do so. But by doing that, you create a reality that is limiting in a Universe that is limitless. My main inspiration for writing this book is to help those who are willing to remember their truest self; To remind them to find alignment with themselves once again, to be able to connect to themselves on a soul level, and operate from this point of view. The idea isn't to tell them how to live, but to help them recall their true identity beyond the logic that a human mind can perceive.

Finding My Passion

Growing up, we experienced financial hardships. We always had problems about not having money to support our basic needs. But one thing that struck me is that when I thought about our problems, I wondered about the reason behind them. Even as a child, I figured on my own through observation that the challenges in our lives existed for a reason—either for the betterment of our lives—or the opposite. I can't remember the exact age; I may have been around eight years old when I realized that problems must exist for us to learn from them.

CHAPTER 6 : PURPOSE

And I now understand that they are, in fact, useful tools for us to grow and understand ourselves better. If we are here to learn from our experiences, maybe after our lives here there will be something more? Maybe there will be someplace next to this life where we can apply what we've learned in this lifetime; something beyond what our eyes can see and our minds can comprehend.

It's not easy to convince yourself to believe in something beyond what the logical mind can understand. You may not immediately get a confirmation from the divine Creator, God, your higher self, or the spirits of passed loved ones that your life here in the physical world is temporary and meant for you to grow and learn. You may need "proof" before you believe. It can be hard to fathom especially because we are always seeking what's "real" and what we consider reasonable in light of what we already know. But notice when you're stuck in a phase and the only thing that assures you that everything will be alright is your ability to hope that things will be... That's when you learn to settle into the idea of believing in that which you cannot see. Often you only lean into your faith as a last resort, because it's the only thing you can hold onto in bad times. Take this example: if one of your friends is going through a tough time and you know that not a single thing you say or do will help that person, you will probably still say, "Everything is going to be okay." Where did you learn that?

It's faith. And you don't have to wait to encounter difficulties to seek faith. You can embrace it any time, even on days when you think you are in control of the situation. Trust in the idea that something greater is out there and it is available for you if you allow it to be.

Going Within

Not everyone finds it easy to believe in the idea that we are eternal beings experiencing this temporary physical life to gain wisdom and grow through love and light. This is understandable. You can still believe that you are here to learn and explore, to get to know yourself, to find and build meaningful relationships. You are here to express your truest desires, to be empowered in what you can become. You are here to enjoy this life despite any challenges you may face. You are here to witness the beauty of nature along with the beauty of your existence. You are here to uncover the truth that has been sitting in front of you your whole life: That you are the creator of your experience and your belief system, your actions and values; that they are your tools in creating your desired path.

And you would not know this to be true to you unless you accept and believe for it to be. When you stop looking for answers outside of yourself, and instead start feeling present in each moment, you begin to open the door to a realm of new perspectives. When you learn to live life with its own sound, and recognize the noise of the world compared to the quiet content voice of your soul, you'll

CHAPTER 6 : PURPOSE

find it easier to disidentify from the mundane outlook that has been established for you. In contrast, you become conscious of your path and identity, giving you time and energy to fill your own cup. This means you can show up in the world with love and can leave a trace of it wherever you go and wherever life takes you. Your mission here is to discover and unfold your truest potential in harmony with the love and light within.

When you become aware that what's visible is not the only thing that is real, that's when you become open to what you don't know. And it's not that these concepts are hidden from you, there are things you don't see unless you allow them to be seen. Nothing will be forced onto you if you are not ready to accept that your physicality as a human being is not all there is. If you observe the beauty of nature diligently, you see how elegant and intricate it is. This can lead you to the conclusion that there is far more action that's been going on beyond what we see. If you observe the vastness of the ocean or the sky, you will begin to understand that something out of human physicality is working to manifest these magnificent creations. It becomes easier to fathom that there is a divine Creator. And when you fully acknowledge that the material world came into existence as a result of divine intervention, you open yourself up to formerly "impossible" possibilities. You understand that an existing divine spirit within you is resonating with the divine which manifested your experiences here. But how will you understand this idea to be true when it's beyond your comprehension? Why do you have faith?

Why do you believe in a reality you can't see? It is because, even if your mind can't grasp the idea of powerful divine manifestation, your heart remembers who you truly are.

If you believe that your purpose is greater than merely fulfilling physical desires or reaching the material goals you've set for yourself, then you understand the concept of a deeper sense of purpose. If you understand the importance of how this inner concept of belief can play out in your life, you will understand that every detail of your life is important, and every seemingly insurmountable problem is small in the grand scope of the Universe. Having faith in something beyond what you can see is like being able to opt out of your problems in the physical world and being able to step back to see that your issues aren't as big as you perceive them to be. If you have problems that you think are crushing you, go to the beach and gaze at the horizon or look up and realize how big the world is and how one problem (no matter how it feels) is still a speck in relation to what is around you.

The Meaning of Your Existence

When someone asks you why we exist, it's usually hard to come up with an immediate answer. It's one of the most difficult questions to answer. You may not have an answer until you reach a point in your life where you've become more conscious, and you have an awareness within yourself and your surroundings. Sometimes, people only answer this

CHAPTER 6 : PURPOSE

question on their deathbed or maybe after fifty years or after an event that leads them to an awakening in life.

It becomes harder when you associate the meaning of your existence to how existence started. We collectively continue to study our origins. We keep looking for answers on how we evolved as humans and how we came about to find and connect the purpose of our individual existence as well. My goal here is to convey that where we came from as physical beings and how we came about is important to know; however, as an individual it's more important to focus on how meaningful your life/existence is to you now. Some people rely on the materials and research of others to arrive at conclusions for themselves, but as long as you're being you (in light and love) it's okay to not know all the answers. The thing is, you already have the answer to every question that feels difficult, you may just be asking the wrong question. Merely shift your perspective to something focused on your involvement in your existence here rather than trying to find the origin of your physical evolution. When you change the question, you go from asking yourself what your purpose is to how you'd like your purpose to be. The focus of your intention shifts you into being the creator of your life.

When you're asked about your purpose in this world, change the question in your mind to how you'd like to contribute in this life. Simplify all the big questions into something you can answer—answers that you can find within yourself without referencing others outside of you. If you ask yourself what the world is asking of you, it's going to be difficult because your self-identification may sabotage you. This is especially the case when you are surrounded by people you perceive to be better than you. The best way to find the meaning of your existence is to ask yourself how you'd like to live in this life.

Next, consider how are you going to contribute in a sustainable way, without depleting yourself? You need to make sure your cup is overflowing, and the overflow is what you're meant to share with others. Make sure you're not prioritizing what the world needs versus what you can give now. Be kind to yourself and find a way to make things less difficult by rephrasing the question to be focused on what you'd like instead of what you think the world wants from you.

The Importance of Thinking for Yourself

Finding your purpose requires mindfulness and optimism. You have to observe your thought patterns so you can always envision the positive outcome. Being realistic is understandable, but if all you see is full of negativity it's not worth dwelling on. For example, if what you see in the news makes you sad and scared, then it's not worth it to continue watching. Instead, step out of that scenario and come up with a thought that is more in your favor. This requires practice, especially if you are someone so used to the noise of the world that it's harder for you to hear your inner voice.

CHAPTER 6 : PURPOSE

Have you noticed that when people write books, they go somewhere quiet or find a place where they can build their own bubble to create original content? There is so much noise in the world right now, you need to create your own bubble so you can connect with yourself; otherwise, you may feel lost. The noise of the world has become part of you now, but it doesn't belong to you. It is part of your experience but not your self-identity.

Pay attention to yourself and how you're showing up to the world. Even at a young age you're already told so many things, you're told to study this and that, to learn about history, and learn about how you should be, and how you should act to follow the rules or how you should be successful so you can be happy. But nobody really taught you how to think for yourself. Nobody told you that you have a say, and your individual ability to think for yourself is better than applying the collective way of thinking applied to your life. The society we belong to as a collective has initiative that is good for the society, but at the end of the day, in order to become a better contributor to the community, we have to feel whole individually first. We exist in a society in which we are judged for being different and that it's better for us to go the common path. But the truth is, you may resonate with others, but each of us are all different from one another. So it's terrible that you are expected to act as one when your perspective is more potent when you nurture your individuality.

Again, the meaning of our existence is subjective, with the only truth being that we all came from love. The rest of your story in this lifetime is up to you and in your hands. So, if you're wondering what the meaning of your existence is right now, then maybe you have to do more self-reflection to really dig into what you think is important to you and live with that meaning. Your perception about the meaning of your existence is exclusive to you. The reason why there's so much division in this world is because most people expect everyone to carry that same perception of something. It will never work because we are meant to discover this life individually, in our own way. Even if you have a spouse or a family, at the end of the day you have your own views that are true to you, and your siblings or your friends don't have to adapt that as their own since they are also meant to have that figured out for themselves. That is why respect and healthy boundaries are crucial for smooth-sailing life and relationships. When you decide what the meaning of your existence is, then make sure it comes from your heart and not from your material perceptions of this life.

There are going to be days where your mood fluctuates, and that is okay. If you are always in one phase, then you won't appreciate the contrast. If you want to have a steady set of emotions, then it's like you're asking to ride a roller coaster without its ups and downs. When you're down, you appreciate being up more—and you will learn more. When you're up, you appreciate it more because of the downfall you experienced. Just imagine going to a theme park, and instead of riding a roller coaster you ride the train. There's a difference.

Living with the Good

If you go back to the beginning of your journey in this physical world, you will somehow observe a view of how you could respond to the world. Because most of us don't remember a memory of when our mom gave birth to us, observe a newborn baby's behavior. Notice how pure they are, that is how you started. You came into existence with so much pureness within that there is nothing you could do to hurt someone. You bring joy, hope, light, and love to those around you. However, growing up you were exposed to the mundane rules, limitations, judgment, biases, and egoistic thoughts that eventually got absorbed into your thought patterns and accepted as your own identity. The sad part is, you are accepting these paradigms unconsciously and sometimes it takes a while before you realize that you are sabotaging your own life with the beliefs that aren't even yours.

In your experiences, there is good and bad. Duality exists to reach neutrality. You can't see what light looks like if you don't experience darkness. You can't recognize a happy state if you don't experience the other end of it, which is sadness. All of these contrasts are happening not for you to identify which is the right thing to do nor the bad thing to avoid. But rather, both exist for you to learn to recognize them in order to help you gravitate toward a life path you're consciously creating. Once you recognize the mere purpose of good and bad, you are now at the state in your life where you understand that you are creating your own reality; therefore, the idea of good and bad liberates you and puts you in a state of neutrality. In this state, you understand that bad things are not all bad, good things are not all good, but how you perceive them is how it's going to be shown to you, and these are presented in your life according to how you believe them to be. However, whether it's good or bad does not matter because you have free will. Everything you come across will be part of your experience, and it's up to you whether it makes you or breaks you.

Take a breakup, for example. Some would see this as something bad; maybe the experience is miserable because of the pain it caused. Maybe the breakup was a bad thing because it made you feel as if you were not good enough or that someone else was better. To most, this is a bad experience, but to others, it could be a good thing. Perhaps due to that difficult breakup, you found yourself and learned to love yourself even more. What if, because of that breakup, you've seen yourself evaluate your life deeply and have clarity on what you truly want. So, even if it was a bad experience to someone, there could still be good points happening around the moment that may only be noticed when the person looks back on their life. What if, because of that breakup, they became more focused on reaching their goals in life? What if, after that breakup, the person finally found happiness on their own? These are possibilities of bad things with good outcomes. However, there are also bad things with bad outcomes. One example is being miserable as a result of the breakup and letting yourself go with sadness to the point that you'd throw your life away to waste because of the bad breakup you experienced. But notice that, whether it's a bad or good experience, your decision whether you'd want for your life to become better or just let yourself be hopeless is up to you. You always have a say as to what happens on the next page. You always have the will to turn things in the direction you want them to be.

Your life experience goes beyond what is good or bad; this is about love and the truth of who you are. Love is within you and within all of what you see. It can't be explained through my perspective alone, but again, can be observed in a newborn baby. This feeling gives you warmth and strength since love is the strongest connection you have, and without love you are not aligned with your true self. Even in people who have done something bad, you can still believe they have something good inside of them. When you open your perception to the concept that we are all vibrating on the high frequency of love, you understand that shocking or horrific circumstances can blind someone of their truth. Some people turn to the absence of love through their circumstances, but they are truly good deep inside as they have love within them, interconnecting with each other, to the Universe and to the divine Creator.

Understanding Life and Love

When you look at your life from a perspective of learning, you won't interpret your circumstances as negative; instead, you'll understand them as guidance to bring you to light. Every one of us want to feel loved and be comforted, accepted, valued, and respected. Why do we share this common desire? It is because our common denominator is our true state. If you want to be happy, it's not because you don't have it within you, it is because you long to be who you are, at your core. You are happiness when you vibrate on the energy of unconditional love. If you find yourself looking outside for happiness, it's because you're focusing on things that are not favorable to you, such as the negativity a problem brings; therefore, you build experiences aligned with the negative energy. When you focus on the loss, you fail to notice the gain. It's easy to get lost in all the tangible labels you use to identify yourself. If you are suffering from depression, it's easier for you to identify as someone who is depressed. Of course, you have the right to see yourself that way, but at the same time, you always have a choice to find a different definition of who you are and what you're experiencing that is more positive and supportive, such as, "I am a person who feels things deeply."

CHAPTER 6 : PURPOSE

If you look at life from a perspective of learning, you see that your experiences act as your guide, but some people never see life as a teacher. They see life as something that they should live to become successful. Life is more than just living and following an established path. It's actually a series of life lessons that we get to learn from. If you see life from this point of view, it's easier for you to get by and find solutions to your problems.

You are here to learn. You are here to enjoy and appreciate the little moments and details of this life experience. You're here to learn about yourself, your life and understand how to show compassion and love to others. You aren't told to get a degree to get a job or to do whatever. As long as you live this life in goodness and light, then you can do whatever you desire to experience. You are part of society and family, yes, but there's nothing wrong with deciding for yourself as long as it's good for you and for other people. You can basically be who you want to be, and be anywhere you want as long as you remain kind, loving, and respectful to yourself and the people around you.

Love as a Guiding Principle

Duality exists to bring you the concept of choice; it forces you to use your judgment to make the best choice in any given moment. As a divine spirit in a physical body, you are meant to experience this life in its fullness through love and light as that is your natural state. Duality plays a role when it comes to making decisions that will lead you to an outcome that is in favor of the good and the goodness in you. There are no rules as to what to do and what not to, but you need to learn to always choose love over anything else. Always choose the good because that is natural to you. That is you. Forgive yourself if you've done something outside of love and give yourself a chance to come back to your natural state. Help yourself by finding love within you and going after experiences that ignite the light in you. Forget about what other people say, do what you desire, and let the energy of love flow naturally within you. Even when you're blinded and see the bad as "good," you will still learn something from it. Always remember to live in accordance with love and express it throughout your lifetime. When you do this, you can expect infinite bliss. Trust me, nothing will come out wrong with love in your actions and love in your heart. Make it your goal to help people see the good in everything and help them see that choosing goodness requires nothing more than allowing it to occur.

Love Is Literally You

Look inward, learn more, and love more. You are love. If you forgot that, this is why you're reading this book. You are love that came into existence because of its magnificent power to manifest physical things. Love is more than just an emotion; it's an energy that lets you vibrate in a very light manner in which you don't have anything to worry about. It's like you're floating over a cloud with pure joy and happiness. Love is not just treating others kindly and showing compassion, love is literally you. If you feel something in your heart while reading these words, your body is agreeing with this truth because that is your truth, too. Don't forget that you're here to expand your loving energy towards anyone in your life, maybe a stranger or someone you don't agree with all the time. It is showing your light to the world and to the rest of those who have forgotten their true essence. The smallest gesture of life that you can control and carry with you all the time is a simple smile. You are here now, as the love you've always been. You have a light within you that you carry with you continually, and no matter how naive or powerless you feel, inside you is a gentle, wise, pure light that is reminding you to take your power back and live it now.

You are powerful in so many ways, but you forgot that you are. You're reading this book to remind you of that lost connection. You're still you, it's just time to reconnect with yourself to get back on track and live your life fully. It's time to awaken to your truth, your light, and the love you've been carrying. There's a divine Creator out there and that divine Creator is part of who you truly are.

What Is Your Purpose?

Your purpose is to experience life. Your purpose is to learn from your experiences. Your purpose is to grow and become a stronger, wiser, and more compassionate person with each struggle you face. And you know what? This is everyone's purpose.

When you love what you do, you are living your purpose. It's as simple as that. You don't have to be a philanthropist to feel secure in the fact that you've done something with a greater purpose. When you look within and learned to live the life you love to experience, that is you, living your purpose. You also have to understand what you truly want in life because only you will comprehend the kind of meaning you give to this life experience.

If you're still struggling to find your purpose, consider tapping into the love and light within you and start from there. Like I said, with love, no outcome will be wrong. Everything will fall into place. At the end of the day, we exist here to spread love by respecting others, rooting for others, growing and learning through our mistakes, being curious, and always remaining open to different perspectives. Our purpose is to learn that we still have more things to learn, and that it is exciting to navigate a life knowing that we are love, and we are the light this world needs.

If we look inward and nurture our own individuality, imagine the amplification if an entire society does this as well. We will live in such harmony that we'll always feel loved, secured, and in bliss. What a wonderful image to imagine, what a wonderful dream we can manifest into reality. It's not the government that needs to change, it's not the community who's to blame, it's us—everything we do is creating and manifesting into a collective reality.

I know it's a bit of a stretch, but you can never limit yourself when you know you can go further. Your true power is not about the potential you have, but about believing in your potential. This serves as fuel to level up your perspective that will bring you wonderful experiences. Your legacy will bring so much light in a world that has been deafened by noise. Your life is worthy of being lived in harmony with your divine Creator and it's worth it to always see yourself from the perspective of a learner to grasp the ideas and have patience to evaluate your challenges as a physical being with a divine spirit. You are powerful and once you leave this planet, you will remember it all.

Stop fueling your worries of the world and start focusing on what you can enjoy, learn, and love in this experience. Try to focus on the lighter side of what this life has to offer. Yes, low vibrations do exist sometimes, but they don't need to stay for good unless you allow them to. Life is temporary but the lessons and the value you share with others will remain, the love you give will multiply. Learn to love in generosity, to offer help in kindness, and to give in pure bliss .

CHAPTER 7
Social & External Factors

PUTTING YOUR AUTHENTIC SELF FIRST

In this chapter, you'll learn valuable ways to embrace who you are— your authentic self. We'll also tackle the importance of your individual role in the community and how your contribution can add value to the lives of others.

It's common to question your abilities when you live in an environment in which you are exposed to so many other people's beliefs and perceptions. When I'm writing, I always think about how others will receive my work. I worry whether my ideas are profound enough to be put out into the world. I even considered not continuing what I started because I didn't think I was good enough to be writing a book. You may think I was full of self-pity or felt incompetent. But what was actually happening is that I started thinking about great authors and what they've accomplished, and I compared myself to where they are in their journey. You see, it's not that I don't believe in myself—I do. But I was bothered by the idea of seeing my potential from the lens of authors who'd already made it. I worried other authors would read this book and not see it as a professional effort. At first glance, it would appear that I have self-esteem issues, but my issue is actually about others' point of views. If I see my work from the point of view of a best-selling author, knowing this is my first book, I'd think it could use some help. But if I see my work from my own lens of where I am now, this has been one of the most rewarding things I've done in my life. So which point of view should I focus on, my own—or that of others?

Because I'm now able to notice when these types of thoughts creep in, I let them sit for a minute then shift into thinking of something that benefits me, and that is understanding that my perception is unique to me. My authenticity can't be channeled by someone else. Even if I'm not a successful author in other people's eyes, it doesn't mean my ideas are not valuable. Just because others don't see the value in my ideas, it doesn't mean they are of no value to me. At the end of the day, how I view it will always be how it is shown to me. All of my ideas are from my own surroundings, experiences, and intuition filtered by my own senses, and nobody can see and think exactly as I do. That's the beauty of perception, each of us has something to offer that is exclusive to us. We don't have to be someone else to shine because we already are shining within.

CHAPTER 7 : SOCIAL & EXTERNAL FACTORS

Once you fully understand who you are, it becomes easier to move forward with your life knowing the truth you have within yourself. It becomes easier to pursue what you want to do without considering how others may view it. When you become connected with yourself and embrace self-awareness, you become so much more confident in every area of your life. It's not that you think you have it all figured out, but because you're now conscious of your purpose, the meaning you give your life, the value you give your relationships, the lessons you get from your struggles, you know that eventually you will figure things out. It may not be right away, but you already know that everything works out for you in the end.

That's not to say there won't be stumbles along the way. After all, we live in a fear-based society. Negativity is the norm: insecurity, division, hopelessness, and scarcity are shown to us every day as if it's normal.

But if you are clear that you have your own unique perspective and you're allowed to see the world according to how you want to perceive it, you will not fall for the projected reality of society. You will set your own perspectives according to how you see the world and the people in it. Once you learn how to disassociate your own thoughts from the noise of the world, you will gain more clarity on which is your belief—versus what others are trying to make you think. Using your senses, you can create clearer boundaries for yourself and you can judge the world according to your point of view and not how society dictates. This is how you take your power back. You are unique. There's nobody exactly like you—you are authentic, and you don't have to go far to understand that you just have to go within.

Self-Validation

There's no need for you to convince anybody else about what you believe. We all have different perspectives, and we each have a uniqueness that is not available to others. Your innate nature is to be a carrier of love and light, and then you have this life experience that offers you lessons that you identify according to your senses. When you try to always do something according to the standard of other people, you will never become successful at it. That's because each of us has different standards and each of us is meant to be successful in our own ways. Yes, you belong to a society. That is why you are predetermined to be a follower of the social standards. You need to learn to set your own standards so you can gauge them according to your own abilities.

Focus on your perspectives, as it is the gauge of your own experience. The reason why most always fall short is that they view their reality from someone else's point of view. You can never achieve a fulfilling life if you base everything on how others see you. Your own opinion of yourself and your surroundings should be what you focus on because that is unique to you. But that doesn't mean disrespecting those who aren't on your side or those who don't agree with you.

This life is about identifying yourself, identifying your point of view, creating boundaries, and showing equal respect to everyone else who doesn't stand with what you believe in. Life is an inside-out. Cultivate the inner side of you and the outside will align with you. When you embrace your authenticity, you become the unstoppable one.

Going Within

You are special—everyone is—but if you don't recognize yourself as special, you never will be. It has to start with you. You have to accept something to be true before it can show up in your reality. For example, if you accept that you are worthless, you will be drawn to experiences that validate this belief. Life here on Earth is so simple, but we make it complicated because we have a notion that it is. But it can be simplified, and if you accept that it can be, it will. Your experiences here is made up of multiple perspectives; in each perspective you get to be in one reality, but your goal is to learn which reality portrays your perspective and which reality is something that you adapt to be yours even if it comes from the outside. That's why it's so important to love yourself. When you can learn to love yourself, it leads to a self-knowledge that leads you to your truth. You'll discover what you believe to be true versus what others tell you to be true. Your life is designed for you to identify your own perspectives and to live your life according to that foundation. Ground yourself with the knowledge that you've found within.

You don't need anyone else to validate you; you only need to accept yourself for who you are. I've noticed that most of the time, we fall down to our knees when we go beyond ourselves to get validation from other people. We want to be seen in order to get approval. To some extent, we are trained to believe that success hinges on other people's recognition. We're influenced to value ourselves based on criteria that were created by society. We are meant to believe that if people look up to us, we are more valuable than the rest. These ideas are reinforced with social media. However, you don't need to live this way. You don't need the approval of others to lead a meaningful life, you only need the love within you and the good intentions you have for humanity.

The Importance of Contributing Positivity and Love

Remember: Your experiences in life mirrors what's going on within. When you are empty within, you can't expect your life to feel whole. But when you're in the dark, you don't have to turn on the light to make it better, you already have that love and light within you. Your inner light can help guide your way in darkness. So much so that you get to the point wherein you contribute positivity, not because that is what you want to contribute, but because that is what you have become. And every time you are being you, you contribute positive energy to other people.

When you shift your focus away from the news, the world still goes on and the events still take place—with or without your attention. There's a difference between acknowledgment and involvement. You can always acknowledge that people are protesting injustice or raging against the government, but you don't have to become involved. When you're not involved, it doesn't mean you don't care, it just means that it's not your priority to focus on things you can't change, and instead, your priority is to change how you respond to it. And by acknowledging that it exists but not becoming part of the protests or the hate, you can step back and consider what kind of reality you want to see in this world.

Your conscious focus is expensive and so valuable. In fact, it can make other people rich. Because the more people are paying attention to someone, maybe a celebrity, the more they become valuable. That's why it is called paying attention because you are paying something when you focus on them. If you're paying attention to someone to feel happy, it's not enough reason to give your power away since you can make yourself happy and you have everything within you to cultivate that happiness. But if you are giving your attention to those things that add value to you, like providing you motivation, knowledge, and growth, then the attention you pay will be fair since you are getting something in return for your focus. It is a good exchange of energy, you give your power away, but you are getting something of value. Be cautious where you invest your energy. It's not that we let others manipulate us, it's just that we let them do it because we are not being careful and conscious. We have to open our eyes and see the truth behind the illusion.

Everyone is going through something in their lives. There's a story behind every judgment you're about to make. Listen to the story first before jumping to a conclusion. There's good in everyone and we all make mistakes. So, try to come from a place of grace.

Embracing Oneself

YOU are enough. If you have truly internalized this concept, you'll never need outside validation. You won't do things to please someone else. You will have good boundaries. You are open to learning new ideas, but it doesn't mean you have to consume external ideas and adopt them as yours. Your experiences are valid enough to form your idea of life. What's true to you isn't necessarily true to others, so you respect others for their ideas. There will be no fight or hate.

You are your perspective, that is who you are. What you believe in has to come from your experiences—and your experiences alone. Practice identifying which beliefs are yours and which are just spoon-fed to you as if they're yours. It's about time to say no to things you don't agree with but always with respect. It's about time to focus on the things that make you who you are.

The way you see things, the way you feel things, and the way you decide for yourself without any influences from other people even to those who are closest to you. You are what you feel. If you continue to practice this, you will live your life in harmony.

CHAPTER 8

Spirituality & Physicality

YOUR PLACE IN THE NATURAL WORLD

In this chapter, we'll look at our connection with nature and its natural abundance. We're also going to tackle spirituality and why it's important to delve into these realms. There comes a time when you become mindful enough to realize how spectacular nature is and how incredibly magnificent the Creator is for bringing this kind of beauty into being. Not only it is beyond magical, but it is so intricate it's hard to believe it's real. Your body is one of these majestic creations. It is connected and one with nature and beyond all that is seen; magnificently created with particular attributes you wouldn't even think possible. Just looking at a glass of water, I'm mesmerized by its substance, transparency, and how it came into being. Not to mention that I'm taking it in with my amazing eyes that let me see!

Your Spiritual Body

Spirituality is innate, but it cannot be seen in plain sight. A person has to allow it to exist by identifying and perceiving it before it can be noticed in someone's experience. Your spirit is your connection to your divine Creator, and each of us are guided by divine grace through that special connection. This is the nonphysical part of you that is nourished by the light and love within. It cannot be seen, but just like your physical features it can be felt. To understand what it feels like, consider the following example... At some point in your life, you've likely experienced giving without expecting anything in return. You've made someone happy just for the sake of it. That warm feeling you get in the simplest act of kindness is the same feeling your spirit generates. Joy, excitement, compassion, hope, unconditional love, and inspiration are innate to you on a soul level. You are a spirit in a physical body who is here to cultivate these emotions into a tangible experience. You are here to witness the feeling of how it unfolds and grows in your day-to-day life. Your soul can feel the energy, so your physical form enables you to broaden that feeling by seeing, touching, hearing, tasting, smelling, creating, and thinking. This is the reason you're here, to perceive and create your path in light. However, it's easy to get lost in the process. You can become too drawn to the superficial aspect of this concrete experience and get carried away by temporary satisfaction. You may cling to only the surface and forget your soul's deepest calling to amplify your

CHAPTER 8: SPIRITUALITY & PHYSICALITY

sincerest intentions and extend it into the material world. Mostly, it goes the other way around. Sometimes you want to achieve a goal to prove yourself to others. You seek success in order to be recognized. When what should have driven you to your achievements was to understand how satisfying it feels to get what you set out for yourself. How passionate it feels to be ambitious and how astounding it is to know that you can dream, and at the same time have the ability to make it real!

Spirituality is the faith of the unseen and the greater power beyond what can be explained in this human experience. There is no exact corollary in this material world because spirituality is beyond what we can see with the human eye. To me, spirituality is a door that opens so I can roam into a realm that is deeply rooted within myself and the deeper purpose in life. I have no words to describe its great impact to me, but writing this book shows how strongly it has influenced me. When I got in touch with my spirituality, all of a sudden, I just started knowing what I know without knowing how. I found myself longing to be surrounded with nature, hugging trees, walking barefoot, and feeling unexplainable belongingness. When I look up to the sky, I feel free and every time I see the moon, I feel secure, guided, and not alone. I started seeing colors more vibrantly, and every detail I notice becomes more and more precise, pristine, and beautiful. Even the stroke of the wind that caresses my skin...I feel as if it's wanting to catch my attention. My vocabulary has broadened as I stumbled upon words I never would've fathomed, such as physicality, consciousness, awakening, collective consciousness, higher-self, but they now are my go-to-words. I now have more control of my life with the clarity I found. It feels like I can jump into a different realm with my imagination and come back to the present moment with a profound understanding of how all of this works. And with this knowledge that I've found within me, I am more equipped to live life in light and love. Also I'm able to help others gain access to the light inside of them that they have forgotten. There is no final phase in discovering spirituality—I know that there is so much more I am meant to learn in the process, and I will continue to embody these lessons in my life and self-expression.

Going Within

You are innately born in love and light, and these have been within you since you were born. This means that you are purely a reflection of the divine Creator, and you emanate both of these qualities in your journey during this physical life. Love is not only an emotion, it is also an energy equal to the divine Creator that gives you the ability to love unconditionally and to have compassion. Light is the voice in you that advises you to always choose the path that is aligned with love. Remember, you have to set an intention to rediscover this within, carve out time for yourself to reflect, meditate, and become more present and mindful. Notice your thought patterns and watch your self-talk.

The kinder you are to yourself, the closer you are to recognizing your truest identity.

The Importance of Love for Your Physical Body

Your physical body is a gift. It is a tool that reflects your inner being and lets you function well in this material world. It is beautifully created in details and proportion to give you a clear sense of this concrete experience on Earth. Your body is an extension of the divine, it is an incredible creation, from head to toe. Sometimes you may fail to acknowledge your body. Loving yourself and your physicality is a good way to show appreciation for the opportunity to be here with tangible senses and be alive in this lifetime.

Listen to your body. Make sure you are taking care of it. Not only because it is yours, but because this is also your borrowed vessel to experience life. Bless your food and water and everything you put in your body. Become mindful of what you take in, be mindful of the thoughts you absorb, and the environment in which you spend time. Your physical form is not only taking in and digesting the food you put in your body; it is also susceptible to absorbing the energy around you. As such, it is important to detoxify from time to time. Your body knows when you're indulging, and it often results in aches and pains. Usually, these exist to signal you to reflect and listen to your body. Sometimes, as a result of being numb, you'll fail to understand that your body is asking for you to pause and reflect on its needs.

Even the shows you watch can influence your physical body. I remember watching a sad movie, and even a few hours later, the heavy energy lingered in me. It triggered the same emotions that I experienced in my own life, making it more of my own. I caught it because I couldn't find any feasible reason for feeling sad on that day. If I was not aware that this could occur, I would have been vibrating in that energy, accepting it as mine. I would have gone on with my day—or maybe even weeks—carrying it until it became real in my experience. From then on, I've become very careful about consuming only that from which I can benefit. Don't let distractions get value from your attention, and instead, opt for activities that give you value. It's smart to be cautious and wise with your actions in order to protect your well-being. Nobody else can protect you better than yourself; others can help, but the comfort of understanding your mental, emotional, spiritual, and physical being is self-mastery at its finest.

The Importance of Nature

At one time in my life, I questioned my belief in religion. There were rough times that I thought I did not deserve to experience, but it happened to me anyway. During those days, I started losing hope and started doubting my faith in the doctrines. But every time I see the ocean, the sky, and how nature coexists with us, I am always reassured in my faith that a divine Creator exists. Observing the beauty of nature always takes me back to believing in that which is beyond what I

CHAPTER 8: SPIRITUALITY & PHYSICALITY

see. Because of your personal struggles, it may be easy to take things in and get weighed down by it emotionally. It's easy to question your faith when nothing seems to be working out for you. But spending quality time observing the details of how nature works always takes me out of victim mode.

Nature has a very special way of comforting us. Do you wonder how and why? You may think it's because of its enticing beauty that calms us or maybe it's because of its diversity that wows us. But there is actually a deeper reason why we feel what we feel when we're out enjoying nature. We feel a sense of belongingness because we are connected with nature along with all of the creation of the divine. Your physical body is one of its forms that is given to you to enable you to perceive this physical world from a unique point of view. Your body is a creation of the divine that you carry with you and along with it, is the scenery that you see, the water that you drink, the water that flows in the river, the body of water composing the planet, and the water that is flowing within you. These are all parts of nature—and so are you. When you look up and see how the sky is vast and unlimited, that is who you are truly within: vast and unlimited.

When you surround yourself with nature, you surround yourself with infinity. Your ideas and creative energy are more potent when you are outside surrounded by the limitless energy of it. Your consciousness is heightened to its highest potential when you embrace nature's boundless possibilities and appreciate your—and its—existence.

The Importance of Miracles

Miracles are the reason we believe in what we can't see. Miracles happen to you in a surprising way and always work in your favor. It's almost as if it lifts you up when you're at your lowest and shows up right when you need it. But what you may not know is miracles only happen if you allow for them to be. The same way what you focus on becomes part of your reality, miracles occur because that is where you place your attention. Just like with what you feel, you're shown experiences equivalent to it, and what you believe in is what is going to show up for you.

In your physical experience, you seek proof first and then try to convince yourself of its realness, which is the opposite of how miracles work. A miracle relies on your trust in the Universe, the divine Creator, manifestation, and also your trust and faith of your beliefs. Magical events don't actualize if you don't believe they can. It's always about what you allow to manifest in your life that will appear. I used to think when I heard the word "miracle" it was a big event that could turn someone's life around. I always associate it with something like winning the lottery or surviving a near-death experience, but now I understand that it doesn't always have to be a big thing. For me, a miracle is waking up every day. Receiving a kind gesture from a stranger when you're feeling grumpy. Getting an uplifting message from someone out of nowhere when you feel alone and troubled. Building friendships that

CHAPTER 8: SPIRITUALITY & PHYSICALITY

last a lifetime, that is a miracle. These could also be the dreams that came true for you. A miracle can also look like those that didn't work out because something better is meant for you. These situations usually don't make sense in the beginning, but when you look back, you will realize it all happened for a reason.

When I was in third grade, I always wanted to have a bicycle. At that time, it was the only thing I wanted. One of my friends owned one, and I learned to ride a bike because of him letting me borrow it. During that summer vacation, I stayed a month away from home where my uncle lived in a city called Maasin. He lived on a different island far away from where my family lived. The room I stayed in with my sister has a big window and every night before going to bed I'd look outside and find the brightest star to make a wish. My only wish back then was to have a bicycle when I returned home. After four weeks, I went home and saw my younger brother very excitedly break the news to me. He told me that we now have a bicycle and showed me where it was. It was an old bicycle. I was so amazed by how my wish came true knowing that my parents couldn't afford to get me one. I asked my mom how we got the bike, and she said that two weeks earlier, there was a drunk man on a bike who came to our house one evening. He asked my mom if he could leave his bicycle because he was too inebriated to ride on it. My mom said yes and thought the man would come back to get it the next day or two, but he never did. That bike became ours and the owner never came back to get it. In just four weeks my wish was granted, and it was indeed a miracle. From this childhood memory, I've learned to never question my ability to make things happen again because I know I'm backed by the Universe and its magic.

Final Thoughts

THE JOURNEY

Your journey doesn't start tomorrow, it is happening now. You have free will to make it as spectacular or as relaxed as you choose. You can do anything—whether you focus on positivity or become obsessed with things that aren't true to your nature (but learn from it to gravitate toward your true calling). It is up to you. You are enough on your own, you can enjoy the company of others, you can enjoy the love you share with others, but at the end of the day your feelings, your happiness, and your choices will always be that which leads you to where you want to be. To expand, grow, and learn from your experiences, this is what your spirit is asking of you. You are not here to become a victim of your struggles; you are here to appreciate what life can offer, with you acting as the creator of your experiences. You are here as a learner of your own life.

If you approach living this way, you will view things from a broader perspective. By developing clarity within yourself, you will nurture a mindset designed to bring out the best. This enables you to understand yourself better, and by doing so, you will also realize that there are still so many things that are out there for you to discover! So many opportunities that suit you are right there, waiting for you. Of course, these experiences will never come about unless you believe that they can happen for you. The right set of beliefs will take you wherever you want, limitlessly. Let your awareness empower you to take your life to the next level. Treat yourself well, so you can do so with others and live in accordance to how you want this experience to be—as opposed to how others expect you to be. Follow that passion you've found within you. Build your dreams and see them happen in real life. Live for the joy life brings, believe in the tangible, and most especially believe in the unseen.

Life is an opportunity to empower yourself with possibilities. The world is a place where you get a chance to turn your dreams into a tangible version. What is good or bad are not as significant, because everything is up to how you perceive things. One thing is for sure though, there is love, and if you identify yourself with it, you are connected to who you truly are and tuned into your divine purpose. Love is the beginning of all there is. It is the answer, it has always been. If you are living a life full of it, your journey itself becomes a source of wonderful manifestations. When you show the world compassion and kindness unconditionally because it's who you are, you are shining a light to others who forget to remember their own truth. By being happy, content, and grateful you give hope to the hopeless. When you are empowered to create a path of your own, you inspire others—especially those who are stuck in a victim mindset and not acting as the creator of their lives. Your presence can give them an example of how to take their power back, by deciding to get to know themselves more, love themselves better, and believe in their own potential.

Your dreams will continue to turn into reality as long as you believe in them. There is no need to worry about how it will unfold; instead, continue to wait patiently and take reasonable action toward it, but don't forget to have fun in the process! Life is meant to be full of fun, excitement, joy, and love. If this isn't your experience of life at the moment, reflect on your situation. To learn how you can turn your life around, it has to come from you, so start by focusing on treating yourself with kindness. Always find yourself being or doing something that ignites these lighthearted feelings in you—whether it's being creative or expressing gratitude for what you already have.

If you are confused, ask yourself the right questions to get to a point of clarity:

- Why am I feeling the way I do?
- How is this hurdle I'm facing relevant to my growth?

No matter how hard or difficult your struggles, try not to get tied up in them. Instead, try to acknowledge and accept that problems exist and it's okay because they present an opportunity to grow. You don't have to focus on the enormity of the challenges you face, you can merely allow them to exist as is. Their impact on you only depends on how you decide to respond. It's funny to say, "don't take things personally," because it's yours, and of course it's personal, but not taking things personally actually works. When you are so invested in the problem itself, you yourself become part of it. If you're inside the box with your problems, you can't see clearly what's outside the box. And usually that's where you find solutions.

Several times when I had serious problems, the more I dwelled on them, the more it made matters worse. It only intensified my feelings of lack. Whereas, if I forget about it for a while and choose to have fun in the moment and focus on what's working, the next thing I know, my problem is solved. It's fascinating how these things work out without you even noticing. You don't even know when you become the resistance in the flow of your life. By accepting that problems can occur, you become less attached to the emotional consequences that come with it. Yes, you would still feel worry, you'd still get hurt or disappointed, but it's when you don't let yourself get sucked in too much that the solutions arise. Train yourself to not focus on lack— on the things you don't have yet—and remind yourself of all of the goals you've accomplished through the years. If you only focus on the things that didn't work, it's harder for you to recognize those that did. So instead, celebrate the things you're proud of and get fueled by those as inspiration to move forward.

If you consider the state of the world these days, it's difficult to ignore the reality that there are so many issues that need to be addressed. Society encourages us to do something to help, but we can only do so much for others. It's not selfish to meet your needs first; it's not wrong to prioritize yourself. The best way to help the community is by practicing accountability with yourself. Becoming a responsible, empowered person and treating others with respect and love, can start within you but ripple out a long way. Learning what is best for you and showing others closest to you how to figure it out for themselves is the best contribution you can offer to help. You're not here to fix what's broken, you're here to live your life in harmony with everyone else around you. If everyone holds onto this belief, one day we'll find out that the biggest problem we had was not the problem itself but the thought of it. Nature is a testament that even with differences, water, rock, soil, flora, and fauna can coexist harmoniously. The differences we experience are normal; however, the thoughts we carry with our differences is what we need to revisit.

Learn to let go of things that no longer work for you. Learn to detach from relationships that are no longer serving you. The same with the old beliefs that are holding you back—let them go and live your life fully. Again and again, nature is silently showing you that it's okay to unbind. It's okay to part from those who don't help you reach your full potential. With mindfulness, you can digest this process by observing the cycles of nature. If there is a dead leaf on a tree, it normally falls for the new one to start blooming. Even with technology nowadays, if you want to download the latest updates you need to have enough memory to do so. You have to remove old files to make room for the new update. Everything that is going on with your life—even in the little things—is metaphorically providing answers. However, you won't recognize these messages unless you become mindful and self-aware.

Since we were young, we were always getting something in exchange for behaving well. We got praised if we did well in school, to a point that we mainly studied to get good grades rather than to learn. There's a "quid-pro-quo" feeling to it all. As adults, many try to do good in this life only because of the concept of karma or being accepted into heaven. But living your life is not about where you are headed once you leave this physical world—it is about being alive now! It's not about the recognition—it's about the value of the journey. It's not about what you get out of this in the future,—it's about what you're feeling now. It is always about that feeling of being here, right now, doing what you want to do and having what you want to have in this moment. The most valuable experience you get out of this ride in life isn't the flips and turns, it's the idea of taking a leap of faith to be on the roller coaster and get in the ride because you want to experience it. It's because you want to know how it feels. You can so get caught up in the things you think you are "supposed" to do that you no longer realize you're complying rather than living. You're chasing after something in order to feel good, when you can make the decision to feel good now, to feel content now, to feel fulfilled and satisfied in this moment.

We all just become stories in the end. In the stories we tell, the material aspect of it all doesn't really matter. What we share with others that transcends beyond the labels of the physical factor are the emotions that came through our experiences. It's not going to be about the big house you bought—it's going to be the perseverance, the faith, and the strength you put into manifesting it. It's not about being an award-winning author—it's about your curiosity to learn; it's about your willingness to share and impart wisdom. It's the courage, the excitement, the joy, the sadness you overcame and the love you shared that matters most. It's not about how much you gave—it's about why you give. Stories with true emotions, these are the ones that change people's lives because your emotion is the most "real" thing you have.

We will continue to gravitate toward people who are true to themselves because that is a sign for us to look within and remember that we are called to do the same. You have a light in you that is waiting to be noticed. Open your senses to it and embrace the truth of who you really are in spirit and live it here and now. You are a form of love, your purpose is to feel it, hear it, and see it on this beautiful, exciting, and multifaceted journey.

ABOUT THE AUTHOR

Shiena Gable believes in the power of self-expression and its potential to carry an energy that brings hope, love, and compassion to one another.

Made in United States
Orlando, FL
29 September 2023